Cram101 Textbook Outlines to accompany:

Social Psychology

Brehm, Kassin, and Fein, 5th Edition

An Academic Internet Publishers (AIPI) publication (c) 2007.

You have a discounted membership at www.Cram101.com with this book.

Get all of the practice tests for the chapters of this textbook, and access in-depth reference material for writing essays and papers. Here is an example from a Cram101 Biology text:

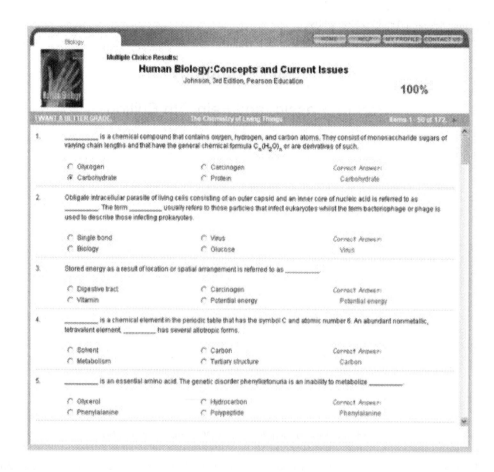

When you need problem solving help with math, stats, and other disciplines, www.Cram101.com will walk through the formulas and solutions step by step.

With Cram101.com online, you also have access to extensive reference material.

You will nail those essays and papers. Here is an example from a Cram101 Biology text:

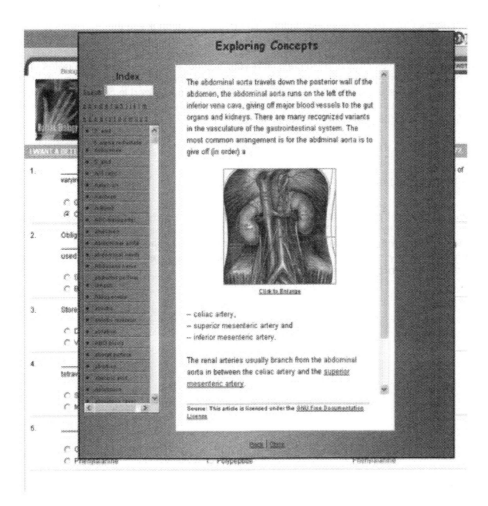

Visit **www.Cram101.com**, click Sign Up at the top of the screen, and enter DK73DW in the promo code box on the registration screen. Access to www.Cram101.com is normally $9.95, but because you have purchased this book, your access fee is only $4.95. Sign up and stop highlighting textbooks forever.

Learning System

Cram101 Textbook Outlines is a learning system. The notes in this book are the highlights of your textbook, you will never have to highlight a book again.

How to use this book. Take this book to class, it is your notebook for the lecture. The notes and highlights on the left hand side of the pages follow the outline and order of the textbook. All you have to do is follow along while your intructor presents the lecture. Circle the items emphasized in class and add other important information on the right side. With Cram101 Textbook Outlines you'll spend less time writing and more time listening. Learning becomes more efficient.

Cram101.com Online

Increase your studying efficiency by using Cram101.com's practice tests and online reference material. It is the perfect complement to Cram101 Textbook Outlines. Use self-teaching matching tests or simulate in-class testing with comprehensive multiple choice tests, or simply use Cram's true and false tests for quick review. Cram101.com even allows you to enter your in-class notes for an integrated studying format combining the textbook notes with your class notes.

Social Psychology
Brehm, Kassin, and Fein, 5th

CONTENTS

Social psychology	Social psychology is the study of the nature and causes of human social behavior, with an emphasis on how people think towards each other and how they relate to each other.
Clique	A clique is an informal and restricted social group formed by a number of people who share common. Social roles vary, but two roles commonly associated with a female clique is notably applicable to most - that of the "queen bee" and that of the "outcast".
Learning	Learning is a relatively permanent change in behavior that results from experience. Thus, to attribute a behavioral change to learning, the change must be relatively permanent and must result from experience.
Intuition	Quick, impulsive thought that does not make use of formal logic or clear reasoning is referred to as intuition.
Humanistic	Humanistic refers to any system of thought focused on subjective experience and human problems and potentials.
Scientific method	Psychologists gather data in order to describe, understand, predict, and control behavior. Scientific method refers to an approach that can be used to discover accurate information. It includes these steps: understand the problem, collect data, draw conclusions, and revise research conclusions.
Attitude	An enduring mental representation of a person, place, or thing that evokes an emotional response and related behavior is called attitude.
Emotion	An emotion is a mental states that arise spontaneously, rather than through conscious effort. They are often accompanied by physiological changes.
Neurotransmitter	A neurotransmitter is a chemical that is used to relay, amplify and modulate electrical signals between a neurons and another cell.
Brain	The brain controls and coordinates most movement, behavior and homeostatic body functions such as heartbeat, blood pressure, fluid balance and body temperature. Functions of the brain are responsible for cognition, emotion, memory, motor learning and other sorts of learning. The brain is primarily made up of two types of cells: glia and neurons.
Affect	A subjective feeling or emotional tone often accompanied by bodily expressions noticeable to others is called affect.
Motives	Needs or desires that energize and direct behavior toward a goal are motives.
Self-esteem	Self-esteem refers to a person's subjective appraisal of himself or herself as intrinsically positive or negative to some degree.
Prejudice	Prejudice in general, implies coming to a judgment on the subject before learning where the preponderance of the evidence actually lies, or formation of a judgement without direct experience.
Variable	A variable refers to a measurable factor, characteristic, or attribute of an individual or a system.
Gender difference	A gender difference is a disparity between genders involving quality or quantity. Though some gender differences are controversial, they are not to be confused with sexist stereotypes.
Clinical psychologist	A psychologist, usually with a Ph.D, whose training is in the diagnosis, treatment, or research of psychological and behavioral disorders is a clinical psychologist.
Anxiety	Anxiety is a complex combination of the feeling of fear, apprehension and worry often accompanied by physical sensations such as palpitations, chest pain and/or shortness of breath.
Psychological disorder	Mental processes and/or behavior patterns that cause emotional distress and/or substantial impairment in functioning is a psychological disorder.
Personality	Personality refers to the pattern of enduring characteristics that differentiates a person, the patterns of behaviors that make each individual unique.

Negative feedback	In negative feedback, the output of a system is added back into the input, so as to reverse the direction of change. This tends to keep the output from changing, so it is stabilizing and attempts to maintain homeostasis.
Feedback	Feedback refers to information returned to a person about the effects a response has had.
Mental processes	The thoughts, feelings, and motives that each of us experiences privately but that cannot be observed directly are called mental processes.
Reasoning	Reasoning is the act of using reason to derive a conclusion from certain premises. There are two main methods to reach a conclusion,deductive reasoning and inductive reasoning.
Social cognition	Social cognition is the name for both a branch of psychology that studies the cognitive processes involved in social interaction, and an umbrella term for the processes themselves. It uses the tools and assumptions of cognitive psychology to study how people understand themselves and others in society and social situations.
Cognition	The intellectual processes through which information is obtained, transformed, stored, retrieved, and otherwise used is cognition.
Social perception	A subfield of social psychology that studies the ways in which we form and modify impressions of others is social perception.
Perception	Perception is the process of acquiring, interpreting, selecting, and organizing sensory information.
Wisdom	Wisdom is the ability to make correct judgments and decisions. It is an intangible quality gained through experience. Whether or not something is wise is determined in a pragmatic sense by its popularity, how long it has been around, and its ability to predict against future events.
Positive reinforcement	In positive reinforcement, a stimulus is added and the rate of responding increases.
Reinforcement	In operant conditioning, reinforcement is any change in an environment that (a) occurs after the behavior, (b) seems to make that behavior re-occur more often in the future and (c) that reoccurence of behavior must be the result of the change.
Theories	Theories are logically self-consistent models or frameworks describing the behavior of a certain natural or social phenomenon. They are broad explanations and predictions concerning phenomena of interest.
Critical thinking	Critical thinking is a mental process of analyzing or evaluating information, particularly statements or propositions that are offered as true.
Conformity	Conformity is the degree to which members of a group will change their behavior, views and attitudes to fit the views of the group. The group can influence members via unconscious processes or via overt social pressure on individuals.
Obedience	Obedience is the willingness to follow the will of others. Humans have been shown to be surprisingly obedient in the presence of perceived legitimate authority figures, as demonstrated by the Milgram experiment in the 1960s.
Social influence	Social influence is when the actions or thoughts of individual(s) are changed by other individual(s). Peer pressure is an example of social influence.
Psychoanalysis	Psychoanalysis refers to the school of psychology that emphasizes the importance of unconscious motives and conflicts as determinants of human behavior. It was Freud's method of exploring human personality.
Behaviorism	The school of psychology that defines psychology as the study of observable behavior and studies relationships between stimuli and responses is called behaviorism. Behaviorism relied heavily on animal research and stated the same principles governed the behavior of both nonhumans and humans.
Physical	Physical attractiveness is the perception of an individual as physically beautiful by other people.

attractiveness	
Research method	The scope of the research method is to produce some new knowledge. This, in principle, can take three main forms: Exploratory research; Constructive research; and Empirical research.
Attention	Attention is the cognitive process of selectively concentrating on one thing while ignoring other things. Psychologists have labeled three types of attention: sustained attention, selective attention, and divided attention.
Attachment	Attachment is the tendency to seek closeness to another person and feel secure when that person is present.
Motivation	In psychology, motivation is the driving force (desire) behind all actions of an organism.
Pluralism	Pluralism refers to the coexistence of distinct ethnic and cultural groups in the same society. Individuals with a pluralistic stance usually advocate that cultural differences be maintained and appreciated.
Social neuroscience	The study of the relationship between neural and social processes is called social neuroscience.
Neuroscience	A field that combines the work of psychologists, biologists, biochemists, medical researchers, and others in the study of the structure and function of the nervous system is neuroscience.
Hormone	A hormone is a chemical messenger from one cell (or group of cells) to another. The best known are those produced by endocrine glands, but they are produced by nearly every organ system. The function of hormones is to serve as a signal to the target cells; the action of the hormone is determined by the pattern of secretion and the signal transduction of the receiving tissue.
Amygdala	Located in the brain's medial temporal lobe, the almond-shaped amygdala is believed to play a key role in the emotions. It forms part of the limbic system and is linked to both fear responses and pleasure. Its size is positively correlated with aggressive behavior across species.
Gene	A gene is an ultramicroscopic area of the chromosome. It is the smallest physical unit of the DNA molecule that carries a piece of hereditary information.
Trait	An enduring personality characteristic that tends to lead to certain behaviors is called a trait. The term trait also means a genetically inherited feature of an organism.
Sexual orientation	Sexual orientation refers to the sex or gender of people who are the focus of a person's amorous or erotic desires, fantasies, and spontaneous feelings, the gender(s) toward which one is primarily "oriented".
Evolution	Commonly used to refer to gradual change, evolution is the change in the frequency of alleles within a population from one generation to the next. This change may be caused by different mechanisms, including natural selection, genetic drift, or changes in population (gene flow).
Ethnic group	An ethnic group is a culture or subculture whose members are readily distinguishable by outsiders based on traits originating from a common racial, national, linguistic, or religious source. Members of an ethnic group are often presumed to be culturally or biologically similar, although this is not in fact necessarily the case.
Collectivist	A person who defines the self in terms of relationships to other people and groups and gives priority to group goals is called collectivist.
Positron emission tomography	Positron Emission Tomography measures emissions from radioactively labeled chemicals that have been injected into the bloodstream. The greatest benefit is that different compounds can show blood flow and oxygen and glucose metabolism in the tissues of the working brain.
Magnetic resonance	Magnetic resonance imaging is a method of creating images of the inside of opaque organs in living organisms as well as detecting the amount of bound water in geological structures. It is primarily used

Go to **Cram101.com** for the Practice Tests for this Chapter.

imaging	to demonstrate pathological or other physiological alterations of living tissues and is a commonly used form of medical imaging.
Social isolation	Social isolation refers to a type of loneliness that occurs when a person lacks a sense of integrated involvement. Being deprived of participation in a group or community involving companionship, shared interests, organized activities, and meaningful roles causes a person to feel alone.

Go to **Cram101.com** for the Practice Tests for this Chapter.

Friendship	The essentials of friendship are reciprocity and commitment between individuals who see themselves more or less as equals. Interaction between friends rests on a more equal power base than the interaction between children and adults.
Wisdom	Wisdom is the ability to make correct judgments and decisions. It is an intangible quality gained through experience. Whether or not something is wise is determined in a pragmatic sense by its popularity, how long it has been around, and its ability to predict against future events.
Social psychology	Social psychology is the study of the nature and causes of human social behavior, with an emphasis on how people think towards each other and how they relate to each other.
Theories	Theories are logically self-consistent models or frameworks describing the behavior of a certain natural or social phenomenon. They are broad explanations and predictions concerning phenomena of interest.
Scientific method	Psychologists gather data in order to describe, understand, predict, and control behavior. Scientific method refers to an approach that can be used to discover accurate information. It includes these steps: understand the problem, collect data, draw conclusions, and revise research conclusions.
Variable	A variable refers to a measurable factor, characteristic, or attribute of an individual or a system.
Human nature	Human nature is the fundamental nature and substance of humans, as well as the range of human behavior that is believed to be invariant over long periods of time and across very different cultural contexts.
Learning	Learning is a relatively permanent change in behavior that results from experience. Thus, to attribute a behavioral change to learning, the change must be relatively permanent and must result from experience.
Research method	The scope of the research method is to produce some new knowledge. This, in principle, can take three main forms: Exploratory research; Constructive research; and Empirical research.
Intuition	Quick, impulsive thought that does not make use of formal logic or clear reasoning is referred to as intuition.
Reasoning	Reasoning is the act of using reason to derive a conclusion from certain premises. There are two main methods to reach a conclusion, deductive reasoning and inductive reasoning.
Applied research	Applied research is done to solve specific, practical questions; its primary aim is not to gain knowledge for its own sake. It can be exploratory but often it is descriptive. It is almost always done on the basis of basic research.
Stimulus	A change in an environmental condition that elicits a response is a stimulus.
Conformity	Conformity is the degree to which members of a group will change their behavior, views and attitudes to fit the views of the group. The group can influence members via unconscious processes or via overt social pressure on individuals.
Hypothesis	A specific statement about behavior or mental processes that is testable through research is a hypothesis.
Generativity	Generativity refers to an adult's concern for and commitment to the well-being of future generations.
Empirical	Empirical means the use of working hypotheses which are capable of being disproved using observation or experiment.
Self-perception	Self-perception theory is an account of attitude change developed by Daryl Bem. It asserts

Go to **Cram101.com** for the Practice Tests for this Chapter.

theory	that we only have that knowledge of our own behavior and its cauzation that another person can have, and that we develop our attitudes by observing our own behavior and concluding what attitudes must have caused them.
Social self	A collective identity that includes interpersonal relationships plus aspects of identity derived from membership in larger, less personal groups based on race, ethnicity, and culture is called the social self.
Attitude	An enduring mental representation of a person, place, or thing that evokes an emotional response and related behavior is called attitude.
Personality	Personality refers to the pattern of enduring characteristics that differentiates a person, the patterns of behaviors that make each individual unique.
Attention	Attention is the cognitive process of selectively concentrating on one thing while ignoring other things. Psychologists have labeled three types of attention: sustained attention, selective attention, and divided attention.
Validity	The extent to which a test measures what it is intended to measure is called validity.
Basic research	Basic research has as its primary objective the advancement of knowledge and the theoretical understanding of the relations among variables . It is exploratory and often driven by the researcher's curiosity, interest or hunch.
Self-esteem	Self-esteem refers to a person's subjective appraisal of himself or herself as intrinsically positive or negative to some degree.
Prejudice	Prejudice in general, implies coming to a judgment on the subject before learning where the preponderance of the evidence actually lies, or formation of a judgement without direct experience.
Social anxiety	A feeling of apprehension in the presence of others is social anxiety.
Anxiety	Anxiety is a complex combination of the feeling of fear, apprehension and worry often accompanied by physical sensations such as palpitations, chest pain and/or shortness of breath.
Operational definition	An operational definition is the definition of a concept or action in terms of the observable and repeatable process, procedures, and appartaus that illustrates the concept or action.
Trial and error	Trial and error is an approach to problem solving in which one solution after another is tried in no particular order until an answer is found.
Construct validity	The extent to which there is evidence that a test measures a particular hypothetical construct is referred to as construct validity.
Construct	A generalized concept, such as anxiety or gravity, is a construct.
Survey	A method of scientific investigation in which a large sample of people answer questions about their attitudes or behavior is referred to as a survey.
Questionnaire	A self-report method of data collection or clinical assessment method in which the individual being studied checks off items on a printed list, answers multiple-choice questions, or writes out answers to essay questions aimed at producing a selfdescription is called questionnaire.
Coding	In senation, coding is the process by which information about the quality and quantity of a stimulus is preserved in the pattern of action potentials sent through sensory neurons to the central nervous system.
Scheme	According to Piaget, a hypothetical mental structure that permits the classification and organization of new information is called a scheme.

Go to **Cram101.com** for the Practice Tests for this Chapter.

Stereotype	A stereotype is considered to be a group concept, held by one social group about another. They are often used in a negative or prejudicial sense and are frequently used to justify certain discriminatory behaviors. This allows powerful social groups to legitimize and protect their dominant position
Interrater reliability	Interrater reliability is the correlation between ratings of two or more raters in a given research study.
Reliability	Reliability means the extent to which a test produces a consistent , reproducible score .
Hormone	A hormone is a chemical messenger from one cell (or group of cells) to another. The best known are those produced by endocrine glands, but they are produced by nearly every organ system. The function of hormones is to serve as a signal to the target cells; the action of the hormone is determined by the pattern of secretion and the signal transduction of the receiving tissue.
Correlational research	Research that examines the relationship between two sets of variables to determine whether they are associated is called correlational research.
Meta-analysis	In statistics, a meta-analysis combines the results of several studies that address a set of related research hypotheses.
Punishment	Punishment is the addtion of a stimulus that reduces the frequency of a response, or the removal of a stimulus that results in a reduction of the response.
Statistics	Statistics is a type of data analysis which practice includes the planning, summarizing, and interpreting of observations of a system possibly followed by predicting or forecasting of future events based on a mathematical model of the system being observed.
Statistic	A statistic is an observable random variable of a sample.
Population	Population refers to all members of a well-defined group of organisms, events, or things.
Random sampling	The selection of participants in an unbiased manner so that each potential participant has an equal possibility of being selected for the experiment is called random sampling.
Correlation coefficient	Correlation coefficient refers to a number from +1.00 to -1.00 that expresses the direction and extent of the relationship between two variables. The closer to 1, the stronger the relationship. The sign, + or -, indicates the direction.
Correlation	A statistical technique for determining the degree of association between two or more variables is referred to as correlation.
Positive correlation	A relationship between two variables in which both vary in the same direction is called a positive correlation.
Physical attractiveness	Physical attractiveness is the perception of an individual as physically beautiful by other people.
Achievement test	A test designed to determine a person's level of knowledge in a given subject area is referred to as an achievement test.
Ethnicity	Ethnicity refers to a characteristic based on cultural heritage, nationality characteristics, race, religion, and language.
Causation	Causation concerns the time order relationship between two or more objects such that if a specific antecendent condition occurs the same consequent must always follow.
Experimental manipulation	The change that an experimenter deliberately produces in a situation under study is called the experimental manipulation.
Random	Assignment of participants to experimental and control groups by chance is called random

assignment	assignment. Random assigment reduces the likelihood that the results are due to preexisiting systematic differences between the groups.
Laboratory setting	Research setting in which the behavior of interest does not naturally occur is called a laboratory setting.
Independent variable	A condition in a scientific study that is manipulated (assigned different values by a researcher) so that the effects of the manipulation may be observed is called an independent variable.
Dependent variable	A measure of an assumed effect of an independent variable is called the dependent variable.
Motivation	In psychology, motivation is the driving force (desire) behind all actions of an organism.
Statistical significance	The condition that exists when the probability that the observed findings are due to chance is very low is called statistical significance.
Internal validity	Internal validity is a term pertaining to scientific research that signifies the extent to which the conditions within a research design were conducive to drawing the conclusions the researcher was interested in drawing.
Control group	A group that does not receive the treatment effect in an experiment is referred to as the control group or sometimes as the comparison group.
Baseline	Measure of a particular behavior or process taken before the introduction of the independent variable or treatment is called the baseline.
Affect	A subjective feeling or emotional tone often accompanied by bodily expressions noticeable to others is called affect.
Experimenter expectancy effects	Experimenter expectancy effects occur when an experimenter's expectations about the results of an experiment affect his or her behavior toward a participant and thereby influence the participant's responses.
External validity	External validity is a term used in scientific research. It signifies the extent to which the results of a study can be applied to circumstances outside the specific setting in which the research was carried out. In other words, it addresses the question "Can this research be applied to 'the real world'?"
Representative sample	Representative sample refers to a sample of participants selected from the larger population in such a way that important subgroups within the population are included in the sample in the same proportions as they are found in the larger population.
Extraneous variables	Variables that are not directly related to the hypothesis under study and that the experimenter does not actively attempt to control are called extraneous variables.
Interpersonal attraction	Interpersonal attraction is the attraction between people which leads to friendships and romantic relationships. Major variables include propinquity, similarity, familiarity, reciprocal liking, and physical attractiveness.
Confederate	Someone who is posing as a participant in an experiment but is actually assisting the experimenter is a confederate.
Obedience	Obedience is the willingness to follow the will of others. Humans have been shown to be surprisingly obedient in the presence of perceived legitimate authority figures, as demonstrated by the Milgram experiment in the 1960s.
Informed consent	The term used by psychologists to indicate that a person has agreed to participate in research after receiving information about the purposes of the study and the nature of the treatments is informed consent. Even with informed consent, subjects may withdraw from any

Go to **Cram101.com** for the Practice Tests for this Chapter.

experiment at any time.

Debriefing   Process of informing a participant after the experiment about the nature of the experiment, clarifying any misunderstanding, and answering any questions that the participant may have concerning the experiment is called debriefing.

Illusion   An illusion is a distortion of a sensory perception.

Brain	The brain controls and coordinates most movement, behavior and homeostatic body functions such as heartbeat, blood pressure, fluid balance and body temperature. Functions of the brain are responsible for cognition, emotion, memory, motor learning and other sorts of learning. The brain is primarily made up of two types of cells: glia and neurons.
Construct	A generalized concept, such as anxiety or gravity, is a construct.
Self-reflection	In Bandura's social cognitive theory, the ability to analyze one's thoughts and actions is referred to as self-reflection.
Motives	Needs or desires that energize and direct behavior toward a goal are motives.
Emotion	An emotion is a mental states that arise spontaneously, rather than through conscious effort. They are often accompanied by physiological changes.
Affect	A subjective feeling or emotional tone often accompanied by bodily expressions noticeable to others is called affect.
Cognition	The intellectual processes through which information is obtained, transformed, stored, retrieved, and otherwise used is cognition.
Self-concept	Self-concept refers to domain-specific evaluations of the self where a domain may be academics, athletics, etc.
Self-esteem	Self-esteem refers to a person's subjective appraisal of himself or herself as intrinsically positive or negative to some degree.
Stimulus	A change in an environmental condition that elicits a response is a stimulus.
Attention	Attention is the cognitive process of selectively concentrating on one thing while ignoring other things. Psychologists have labeled three types of attention: sustained attention, selective attention, and divided attention.
Body image	A person's body image is their perception of their physical appearance. It is more than what a person thinks they will see in a mirror, it is inextricably tied to their self-esteem and acceptance by peers.
Reflection	Reflection is the process of rephrasing or repeating thoughts and feelings expressed, making the person more aware of what they are saying or thinking.
Species	Species refers to a reproductively isolated breeding population.
Evolution	Commonly used to refer to gradual change, evolution is the change in the frequency of alleles within a population from one generation to the next. This change may be caused by different mechanisms, including natural selection, genetic drift, or changes in population (gene flow).
Social self	A collective identity that includes interpersonal relationships plus aspects of identity derived from membership in larger, less personal groups based on race, ethnicity, and culture is called the social self.
Introspection	Introspection is the self report or consideration of one's own thoughts, perceptions and mental processes. Classic introspection was done through trained observers.
Insight	Insight refers to a sudden awareness of the relationships among various elements that had previously appeared to be independent of one another.
Attitude	An enduring mental representation of a person, place, or thing that evokes an emotional response and related behavior is called attitude.
Meditation	Meditation usually refers to a state in which the body is consciously relaxed and the mind is allowed to become calm and focused.
Psychotherapy	Psychotherapy is a set of techniques based on psychological principles intended to improve

mental health, emotional or behavioral issues.

Dream analysis	Dream analysis is a part of psychoanalysis that intends to look beneath the manifest content of a dream, i.e., what we perceive in the dream, to the latent content of a dream, i.e., the meaning of the dream and the reason we dreamt it.
Hypnosis	Hypnosis is a psychological state whose existence and effects are strongly debated. Some believe that it is a state under which the subject's mind becomes so suggestible that the hypnotist, the one who induces the state, can establish communication with the subconscious mind of the subject and command behavior that the subject would not choose to perform in a conscious state.
Affective forecasting	Affective forecasting is the forecasting of one's emotional state in the future. This kind of prediction is affected by various kinds of cognitive biases, i.e. systematic errors of thought.
Affective	Affective is the way people react emotionally, their ability to feel another living thing's pain or joy.
Self-perception theory	Self-perception theory is an account of attitude change developed by Daryl Bem. It asserts that we only have that knowledge of our own behavior and its cauzation that another person can have, and that we develop our attitudes by observing our own behavior and concluding what attitudes must have caused them.
Punishment	Punishment is the addtion of a stimulus that reduces the frequency of a response, or the removal of a stimulus that results in a reduction of the response.
Personality	Personality refers to the pattern of enduring characteristics that differentiates a person, the patterns of behaviors that make each individual unique.
Subjective experience	Subjective experience refers to reality as it is perceived and interpreted, not as it exists objectively.
Hypothesis	A specific statement about behavior or mental processes that is testable through research is a hypothesis.
Control group	A group that does not receive the treatment effect in an experiment is referred to as the control group or sometimes as the comparison group.
Physiological changes	Alterations in heart rate, blood pressure, perspiration, and other involuntary responses are physiological changes.
Expressive behaviors	Behaviors that express or communicate emotion or personal feelings are expressive behaviors.
Feedback	Feedback refers to information returned to a person about the effects a response has had.
Intuition	Quick, impulsive thought that does not make use of formal logic or clear reasoning is referred to as intuition.
Motivation	In psychology, motivation is the driving force (desire) behind all actions of an organism.
Extrinsic motivation	Responding to external incentives such as rewards and punishments is form of extrinsic motivation. Traditionally, extrinsic motivation has been used to motivate employees: Payments, rewards, control, or punishments.
Intrinsic motivation	Intrinsic motivation causes people to engage in an activity for its own sake. They are subjective factors and include self-determination, curiosity, challenge, effort, and others.
Overjustific-tion effect	The overjustification effect is the effect of giving someone an incentive (monetary or otherwise) to do something that they already enjoy doing. As a result, the person may then view his or her actions as externally controlled rather than intrinsically appealing.

22

Go to **Cram101.com** for the Practice Tests for this Chapter.

Incentive	An incentive is what is expected once a behavior is performed. An incentive acts as a reinforcer.
Social comparison theory	Social comparison theory is the idea that individuals learn about and assess themselves by comparison with other people. Social psychological research shows that individuals tend to lean more toward social comparisons in situations that are ambiguous.
Social comparison	Social comparison theory is the idea that individuals learn about and assess themselves by comparison with other people. Research shows that individuals tend to lean more toward social comparisons in situations that are ambiguous.
Two-factor theory of emotion	Schachter and Singer's two-factor theory of emotion states that emotion is determined by two main factors: physiological arousal and cognitive labeling. Cognitions are used to interpret the meaning of physiological arousal in a particular situation.
Epinephrine	Epinephrine is a hormone and a neurotransmitter. Epinephrine plays a central role in the short-term stress reaction—the physiological response to threatening or exciting conditions. It is secreted by the adrenal medulla. When released into the bloodstream, epinephrine binds to multiple receptors and has numerous effects throughout the body.
Placebo	Placebo refers to a bogus treatment that has the appearance of being genuine.
Confederate	Someone who is posing as a participant in an experiment but is actually assisting the experimenter is a confederate.
Questionnaire	A self-report method of data collection or clinical assessment method in which the individual being studied checks off items on a printed list, answers multiple-choice questions, or writes out answers to essay questions aimed at producing a selfdescription is called questionnaire.
Reasoning	Reasoning is the act of using reason to derive a conclusion from certain premises. There are two main methods to reach a conclusion,deductive reasoning and inductive reasoning.
Passionate love	A state of intense absorption includes intense physiological arousal, psychological interest, and caring for the needs of another is referred to as passionate love.
Adolescence	The period of life bounded by puberty and the assumption of adult responsibilities is adolescence.
Autobiograph-cal memory	An Autobiographical Memory is a personal representation of general or specific events and personal facts.
Psychiatrist	A psychiatrist is a physician who specializes in the diagnosis and treatment of psychological disorders.
Maturation	The orderly unfolding of traits, as regulated by the genetic code is called maturation.
Individualism	Individualism refers to putting personal goals ahead of group goals and defining one's identity in terms of personal attributes rather than group memberships.
Autonomy	Autonomy is the condition of something that does not depend on anything else.
Collectivism	Collectivism is an emphasis on the group, as opposed to the individual. It is syndrome of attitudes and behaviors based on the belief that the basic unit of survival lies within a group, not the individual.
Interdependence	Interdependence is a dynamic of being mutually responsible to and dependent on others.
Collectivist	A person who defines the self in terms of relationships to other people and groups and gives priority to group goals is called collectivist.
Trait	An enduring personality characteristic that tends to lead to certain behaviors is called a

trait. The term trait also means a genetically inherited feature of an organism.

Conformity	Conformity is the degree to which members of a group will change their behavior, views and attitudes to fit the views of the group. The group can influence members via unconscious processes or via overt social pressure on individuals.
Self-image	A person's self-image is the mental picture, generally of a kind that is quite resistant to change, that depicts not only details that are potentially available to objective investigation by others, but also items that have been learned by that person about himself or herself.
Anxiety	Anxiety is a complex combination of the feeling of fear, apprehension and worry often accompanied by physical sensations such as palpitations, chest pain and/or shortness of breath.
Immune system	The most important function of the human immune system occurs at the cellular level of the blood and tissues. The lymphatic and blood circulation systems are highways for specialized white blood cells. These cells include B cells, T cells, natural killer cells, and macrophages. All function with the primary objective of recognizing, attacking and destroying bacteria, viruses, cancer cells, and all substances seen as foreign.
Population	Population refers to all members of a well-defined group of organisms, events, or things.
Gender difference	A gender difference is a disparity between genders involving quality or quantity. Though some gender differences are controversial, they are not to be confused with sexist stereotypes.
Ego	In Freud's view the Ego serves to balance our primitive needs and our moral beliefs and taboos. Relying on experience, a healthy Ego provides the ability to adapt to reality and interact with the outside world.
Statistics	Statistics is a type of data analysis which practice includes the planning, summarizing, and interpreting of observations of a system possibly followed by predicting or forecasting of future events based on a mathematical model of the system being observed.
Statistic	A statistic is an observable random variable of a sample.
Prejudice	Prejudice in general, implies coming to a judgment on the subject before learning where the preponderance of the evidence actually lies, or formation of a judgement without direct experience.
Discrimination	In Learning theory, discrimination refers the ability to distinguish between a conditioned stimulus and other stimuli. It can be brought about by extensive training or differential reinforcement. In social terms, it is the denial of privileges to a person or a group on the basis of prejudice.
Perception	Perception is the process of acquiring, interpreting, selecting, and organizing sensory information.
Self-awareness	Realization that one's existence and functioning are separate from those of other people and things is called self-awareness.
Alcoholism	A disorder that involves long-term, repeated, uncontrolled, compulsive, and excessive use of alcoholic beverages and that impairs the drinker's health and work and social relationships is called alcoholism.
Field study	Field study refers to any scientific research study in which data are collected in a setting other than the laboratory.
Stereotype	A stereotype is considered to be a group concept, held by one social group about another. They are often used in a negative or prejudicial sense and are frequently used to justify certain discriminatory behaviors. This allows powerful social groups to legitimize and protect their

Go to **Cram101.com** for the Practice Tests for this Chapter.

	dominant position
Sexual masochism	Sexual masochism is a preference for obtaining or increasing sexual gratification through subjection of the self to pain or humiliation.
Masochism	The counterpart of sadism is masochism, the sexual pleasure or gratification of having pain or suffering inflicted upon the self, often consisting of sexual fantasies or urges for being beaten, humiliated, bound, tortured, or otherwise made to suffer, either as an enhancement to or a substitute for sexual pleasure.
Ecstasy	Ecstasy as an emotion is to be outside oneself, in a trancelike state in which an individual transcends ordinary consciousness and as a result has a heightened capacity for exceptional thought or experience. Ecstasy also refers to a relatively new hallucinogen that is chemically similar to mescaline and the amphetamines.
Binge	Binge refers to relatively brief episode of uncontrolled, excessive consumption.
Suicide	Suicide behavior is rare in childhood but escalates in adolescence. The suicide rate increases in a linear fashion from adolescence through late adulthood.
Alcoholic	An alcoholic is dependent on alcohol as characterized by craving, loss of control, physical dependence and withdrawal symptoms, and tolerance.
Public self-consciousness	Intense awareness of oneself as a social object is public self-consciousness.
Norms	In testing, standards of test performance that permit the comparison of one person's score on the test to the scores of others who have taken the same test are referred to as norms.
Chronic	Chronic refers to a relatively long duration, usually more than a few months.
Consciousness	The awareness of the sensations, thoughts, and feelings being experienced at a given moment is called consciousness.
Reflex	A simple, involuntary response to a stimulus is referred to as reflex. Reflex actions originate at the spinal cord rather than the brain.
Illusion	An illusion is a distortion of a sensory perception.
Theories	Theories are logically self-consistent models or frameworks describing the behavior of a certain natural or social phenomenon. They are broad explanations and predictions concerning phenomena of interest.
Shyness	A tendency to avoid others plus uneasiness and strain when socializing is called shyness.
Trauma	Trauma refers to a severe physical injury or wound to the body caused by an external force, or a psychological shock having a lasting effect on mental life.
Testosterone	Testosterone is a steroid hormone from the androgen group. It is the principal male sex hormone and the "original" anabolic steroid.
Hormone	A hormone is a chemical messenger from one cell (or group of cells) to another. The best known are those produced by endocrine glands, but they are produced by nearly every organ system. The function of hormones is to serve as a signal to the target cells; the action of the hormone is determined by the pattern of secretion and the signal transduction of the receiving tissue.
Downward social comparison	The defensive tendency to compare ourselves with others who are worse off than we are is called downward social comparison.
Script	A schema, or behavioral sequence, for an event is called a script. It is a form of schematic organization, with real-world events organized in terms of temporal and causal relations

Go to **Cram101.com** for the Practice Tests for this Chapter.

Go to **Cram101.com** for the Practice Tests for this Chapter.
And, **NEVER** highlight a book again!

between component acts.

Social identity	Social identity is the way we define ourselves in terms of group membership.
Ingratiation	Ingratiation is a technique for gaining compliance in which a requester first induces the target person to like them, then attempts to change their behavior in some desired manner.
Eating disorders	Psychological disorders characterized by distortion of the body image and gross disturbances in eating patterns are called eating disorders.
Amphetamine	Amphetamine is a synthetic stimulant used to suppress the appetite, control weight, and treat disorders including narcolepsy and ADHD. It is also used recreationally and for performance enhancement.
Personality trait	According to the Diagnostic and Statistical Manual of the American Psychiatric Association, a personality trait is a "prominent aspect of personality that is exhibited in a wide range of important social and personal contexts. ...".
Social norm	A social norm, is a rule that is socially enforced. In social situations, such as meetings, they are unwritten and often unstated rules that govern individuals' behavior. A social norm is most evident when not followed or broken.
Social psychology	Social psychology is the study of the nature and causes of human social behavior, with an emphasis on how people think towards each other and how they relate to each other.
Survey	A method of scientific investigation in which a large sample of people answer questions about their attitudes or behavior is referred to as a survey.

Stimulant	A stimulant is a drug which increases the activity of the sympathetic nervous system and produces a sense of euphoria or awakeness.
Punishment	Punishment is the addtion of a stimulus that reduces the frequency of a response, or the removal of a stimulus that results in a reduction of the response.
Social perception	A subfield of social psychology that studies the ways in which we form and modify impressions of others is social perception.
Perception	Perception is the process of acquiring, interpreting, selecting, and organizing sensory information.
Self-fulfilling prophecy	A self-fulfilling prophecy is a prediction that, in being made, actually causes itself to become true.
Personality	Personality refers to the pattern of enduring characteristics that differentiates a person, the patterns of behaviors that make each individual unique.
Motives	Needs or desires that energize and direct behavior toward a goal are motives.
Phrenology	Phrenology is a theory which claims to be able to determine character, personality traits, and criminality on the basis of the shape of the head (reading "bumps"). Developed by Gall around 1800, and very popular in the 19th century, it is now discredited as a pseudoscience.
Attention	Attention is the cognitive process of selectively concentrating on one thing while ignoring other things. Psychologists have labeled three types of attention: sustained attention, selective attention, and divided attention.
Trait	An enduring personality characteristic that tends to lead to certain behaviors is called a trait. The term trait also means a genetically inherited feature of an organism.
Script	A schema, or behavioral sequence, for an event is called a script. It is a form of schematic organization, with real-world events organized in terms of temporal and causal relations between component acts.
Emotion	An emotion is a mental states that arise spontaneously, rather than through conscious effort. They are often accompanied by physiological changes.
Species	Species refers to a reproductively isolated breeding population.
Hypothesis	A specific statement about behavior or mental processes that is testable through research is a hypothesis.
Nonverbal communication	Communication between individuals that does not involve the content of spoken language, but relies instead on an unspoken language of facial expressions, eye contact, and body language is nonverbal communication.
Friendship	The essentials of friendship are reciprocity and commitment between individuals who see themselves more or less as equals. Interaction between friends rests on a more equal power base than the interaction between children and adults.
Socioeconomic Status	A family's socioeconomic status is based on family income, parental education level, parental occupation, and social status in the community. Those with high status often have more success in preparing their children for school because they have access to a wide range of resources.
Socioeconomic	Socioeconomic pertains to the study of the social and economic impacts of any product or service offering, market intervention or other activity on an economy as a whole and on the companies, organization and individuals who are its main economic actors.
Norms	In testing, standards of test performance that permit the comparison of one person's score on the test to the scores of others who have taken the same test are referred to as norms.

Go to **Cram101.com** for the Practice Tests for this Chapter.

Habit	A habit is a response that has become completely separated from its eliciting stimulus. Early learning theorists used the term to describe S-R associations, however not all S-R associations become a habit, rather many are extinguished after reinforcement is withdrawn.
Sexual harassment	Deliberate or repeated verbal comments, gestures, or physical contact of a sexual nature that is unwanted by the recipient is called sexual harassment.
Psychoanalysis	Psychoanalysis refers to the school of psychology that emphasizes the importance of unconscious motives and conflicts as determinants of human behavior. It was Freud's method of exploring human personality.
Psychiatrist	A psychiatrist is a physician who specializes in the diagnosis and treatment of psychological disorders.
Attitude	An enduring mental representation of a person, place, or thing that evokes an emotional response and related behavior is called attitude.
Heredity	Heredity is the transfer of characteristics from parent to offspring through their genes.
Attribution theory	Attribution theory is concerned with the ways in which people explain the behavior of others. It explores how individuals "attribute" causes to events and how this cognitive perception affects their motivation.
Concussion	Concussion, or mild traumatic brain injury (MTBI), is the most common and least serious type of brain injury. A milder type of diffuse axonal injury, concussion involves a transient loss of mental function. It can be caused by acceleration or deceleration forces, by a direct blow, or by penetrating injuries.
Situational attribution	Situational attribution refers to an assumption that a person's behavior is determined by external circumstances such as social pressure.
Theories	Theories are logically self-consistent models or frameworks describing the behavior of a certain natural or social phenomenon. They are broad explanations and predictions concerning phenomena of interest.
Inference	Inference is the act or process of drawing a conclusion based solely on what one already knows.
Social role	Social role refers to expected behavior patterns associated with particular social positions.
Variable	A variable refers to a measurable factor, characteristic, or attribute of an individual or a system.
Stimulus	A change in an environmental condition that elicits a response is a stimulus.
Motivation	In psychology, motivation is the driving force (desire) behind all actions of an organism.
Availability heuristic	The availability heuristic is a rule of thumb, or heuristic, which occurs when people estimate the probability of an outcome based on how easy that outcome is to imagine.
Heuristic	A heuristic is a simple, efficient rule of thumb proposed to explain how people make decisions, come to judgments and solve problems, typically when facing complex problems or incomplete information. These rules work well under most circumstances, but in certain cases lead to systematic cognitive biases.
False-consensus effect	The tendency for people to overestimate the extent to which others share their opinions, attributes, and behaviors is called the false-consensus effect.
Personality test	A personality test aims to describe aspects of a person's character that remain stable across situations.
Statistics	Statistics is a type of data analysis which practice includes the planning, summarizing, and

	interpreting of observations of a system possibly followed by predicting or forecasting of future events based on a mathematical model of the system being observed.
Statistic	A statistic is an observable random variable of a sample.
Counterfactual thinking	The tendency to imagine alternative events or outcomes that might have occurred but did not is referred to as counterfactual thinking.
Social psychology	Social psychology is the study of the nature and causes of human social behavior, with an emphasis on how people think towards each other and how they relate to each other.
Fundamental attribution error	The fundamental attribution error is the tendency for people to over-emphasize dispositional, or personality-based, explanations for behaviors observed in others while under-emphasizing the role and power of situational influences on the same behavior.
Reflection	Reflection is the process of rephrasing or repeating thoughts and feelings expressed, making the person more aware of what they are saying or thinking.
Survey	A method of scientific investigation in which a large sample of people answer questions about their attitudes or behavior is referred to as a survey.
Reflex	A simple, involuntary response to a stimulus is referred to as reflex. Reflex actions originate at the spinal cord rather than the brain.
Insight	Insight refers to a sudden awareness of the relationships among various elements that had previously appeared to be independent of one another.
Optical illusion	An optical illusion is any illusion that deceives the human visual system into perceiving something that is not present or incorrectly perceiving what is present. There are physiological illusions and cognitive illusions.
Illusion	An illusion is a distortion of a sensory perception.
Individualist	A person who defines the self in terms of personal traits and gives priority to personal goals is an individualist.
Collectivist	A person who defines the self in terms of relationships to other people and groups and gives priority to group goals is called collectivist.
Self-esteem	Self-esteem refers to a person's subjective appraisal of himself or herself as intrinsically positive or negative to some degree.
Social skills	Social skills are skills used to interact and communicate with others to assist status in the social structure and other motivations.
Confederate	Someone who is posing as a participant in an experiment but is actually assisting the experimenter is a confederate.
Information integration theory	Information integration theory suggests that impressions are based on the disposition of the perceiver, and a weighted average of a target person's traits.
Feedback	Feedback refers to information returned to a person about the effects a response has had.
Priming	A phenomenon in which exposure to a word or concept later makes it easier to recall related information, even when one has no conscious memory of the word or concept is called priming.
Achievement motivation	The psychological need in humans for success is called achievement motivation.
Control group	A group that does not receive the treatment effect in an experiment is referred to as the control group or sometimes as the comparison group.

Extroversion	Extroversion refers to the tendency to be outgoing, adaptable, and sociable.
Agreeableness	Agreeableness, one of the big-five personality traits, reflects individual differences in concern with cooperation and social harmony. It is the degree individuals value getting along with others.
Conscientiou-ness	Conscientiousness is one of the dimensions of the five-factor model of personality and individual differences involving being organized, thorough, and reliable as opposed to careless, negligent, and unreliable.
Valence	In expectancy theory, the value or worth a person gives to an outcome is called the valence.
Brain	The brain controls and coordinates most movement, behavior and homeostatic body functions such as heartbeat, blood pressure, fluid balance and body temperature. Functions of the brain are responsible for cognition, emotion, memory, motor learning and other sorts of learning. The brain is primarily made up of two types of cells: glia and neurons.
Central trait	Gordon Allport delineated different kinds of traits, which he also called dispositions. A Central trait is basic to an individual's personality, while secondary traits are more peripheral. Common traits are those recognized within a culture and thus may vary from culture to culture. Cardinal traits are those by which an individual may be strongly recognized.
Primacy effect	The primacy effect is a cognitive bias that results from disproportionate salience of initial stimuli or observations. If, for example, a subject reads a sufficiently-long list of words, he or she is more likely to remember words read toward the beginning than words read in the middle.
Stereotype	A stereotype is considered to be a group concept, held by one social group about another. They are often used in a negative or prejudicial sense and are frequently used to justify certain discriminatory behaviors. This allows powerful social groups to legitimize and protect their dominant position
Achievement test	A test designed to determine a person's level of knowledge in a given subject area is referred to as an achievement test.
Correlation	A statistical technique for determining the degree of association between two or more variables is referred to as correlation.
Belief perseverance	The tendency to hold on to a belief in the face of contradictory evidence is called belief perseverance.
Introvert	Introvert refers to a person whose attention is focused inward; a shy, reserved, timid person.
Extrovert	Extrovert refers to a person whose attention is directed outward; a bold, outgoing person.
Psychotherapy	Psychotherapy is a set of techniques based on psychological principles intended to improve mental health, emotional or behavioral issues.
Depression	In everyday language depression refers to any downturn in mood, which may be relatively transitory and perhaps due to something trivial. This is differentiated from Clinical depression which is marked by symptoms that last two weeks or more and are so severe that they interfere with daily living.
Human nature	Human nature is the fundamental nature and substance of humans, as well as the range of human behavior that is believed to be invariant over long periods of time and across very different cultural contexts.
Self-concept	Self-concept refers to domain-specific evaluations of the self where a domain may be academics, athletics, etc.

Go to **Cram101.com** for the Practice Tests for this Chapter.

Evolution	Commonly used to refer to gradual change, evolution is the change in the frequency of alleles within a population from one generation to the next. This change may be caused by different mechanisms, including natural selection, genetic drift, or changes in population (gene flow).
Prejudice	Prejudice in general, implies coming to a judgment on the subject before learning where the preponderance of the evidence actually lies, or formation of a judgement without direct experience.
Discrimination	In Learning theory, discrimination refers the ability to distinguish between a conditioned stimulus and other stimuli. It can be brought about by extensive training or differential reinforcement. In social terms, it is the denial of privileges to a person or a group on the basis of prejudice.
Incentive	An incentive is what is expected once a behavior is performed. An incentive acts as a reinforcer.

Go to **Cram101.com** for the Practice Tests for this Chapter.
And, **NEVER** highlight a book again!

Stereotype	A stereotype is considered to be a group concept, held by one social group about another.They are often used in a negative or prejudicial sense and are frequently used to justify certain discriminatory behaviors. This allows powerful social groups to legitimize and protect their dominant position
Prejudice	Prejudice in general, implies coming to a judgment on the subject before learning where the preponderance of the evidence actually lies, or formation of a judgement without direct experience.
Sexism	Sexism is commonly considered to be discrimination against people based on their sex rather than their individual merits, but can also refer to any and all differentiations based on
Discrimination	In Learning theory, discrimination refers the ability to distinguish between a conditioned stimulus and other stimuli. It can be brought about by extensive training or differential reinforcement. In social terms, it is the denial of privileges to a person or a group on the basis of prejudice.
Perception	Perception is the process of acquiring, interpreting, selecting, and organizing sensory information.
Sexual orientation	Sexual orientation refers to the sex or gender of people who are the focus of a person's amorous or erotic desires, fantasies, and spontaneous feelings, the gender(s) toward which one is primarily "oriented".
Trait	An enduring personality characteristic that tends to lead to certain behaviors is called a trait. The term trait also means a genetically inherited feature of an organism.
Sociocultural perspective	The view that focuses on the roles of ethnicity, gender, culture, and socioeconomic status in personality formation, behavior, and mental processes is a sociocultural perspective.
Ingroup	An ingroup is a social group towards which an individual feels loyalty and respect, usually due to membership in the group. This loyalty often manifests itself as an ingroup bias.
Species	Species refers to a reproductively isolated breeding population.
Social categorization	Social categorization refers to the tendency to divide the social world into two separate categories: one's in-group and various out-groups.
Attention	Attention is the cognitive process of selectively concentrating on one thing while ignoring other things. Psychologists have labeled three types of attention: sustained attention, selective attention, and divided attention.
Representative sample	Representative sample refers to a sample of participants selected from the larger population in such a way that important subgroups within the population are included in the sample in the same proportions as they are found in the larger population.
Norms	In testing, standards of test performance that permit the comparison of one person's score on the test to the scores of others who have taken the same test are referred to as norms.
Affect	A subjective feeling or emotional tone often accompanied by bodily expressions noticeable to others is called affect.
Learning	Learning is a relatively permanent change in behavior that results from experience. Thus, to attribute a behavioral change to learning, the change must be relatively permanent and must result from experience.
Confirmation bias	Confirmation bias refers to the tendency to search for and use information that supports, rather than refutes, our ideas.
Attitude	An enduring mental representation of a person, place, or thing that evokes an emotional response and related behavior is called attitude.

Go to **Cram101.com** for the Practice Tests for this Chapter.

Stimulus	A change in an environmental condition that elicits a response is a stimulus.
Contrast effect	A contrast effect is the enhancement or diminishment, relative to normal, of a perception and related performance as a result of immediately previous or simultaneous exposure to a stimulus of lesser or greater value in the same dimension.
Sensation	Sensation is the first stage in the chain of biochemical and neurologic events that begins with the impinging of a stimulus upon the receptor cells of a sensory organ, which then leads to perception, the mental state that is reflected in statements like "I see a uniformly blue wall."
Gender stereotypes	Broad categories that reflect our impressions and beliefs about typical females and males are referred to as gender stereotypes.
Variable	A variable refers to a measurable factor, characteristic, or attribute of an individual or a system.
Fundamental attribution error	The fundamental attribution error is the tendency for people to over-emphasize dispositional, or personality-based, explanations for behaviors observed in others while under-emphasizing the role and power of situational influences on the same behavior.
Motives	Needs or desires that energize and direct behavior toward a goal are motives.
Social perception	A subfield of social psychology that studies the ways in which we form and modify impressions of others is social perception.
Self-fulfilling prophecy	A self-fulfilling prophecy is a prediction that, in being made, actually causes itself to become true.
Controlled processes	Controlled processes refer to the most alert states of consciousness.
Self-esteem	Self-esteem refers to a person's subjective appraisal of himself or herself as intrinsically positive or negative to some degree.
Intelligence test	An intelligence test is a standardized means of assessing a person's current mental ability, for example, the Stanford-Binet test and the Wechsler Adult Intelligence Scale.
Emotion	An emotion is a mental states that arise spontaneously, rather than through conscious effort. They are often accompanied by physiological changes.
Suppression	Suppression is the defense mechanism where a memory is deliberately forgotten.
Hypothesis	A specific statement about behavior or mental processes that is testable through research is a hypothesis.
Motivation	In psychology, motivation is the driving force (desire) behind all actions of an organism.
Biological rhythm	A biological rhythm is a hypothetical cyclic pattern of alterations in physiology, emotions, and/or intellect
Random assignment	Assignment of participants to experimental and control groups by chance is called random assignment. Random assigment reduces the likelihood that the results are due to preexisiting systematic differences between the groups.
Individuating information	Individuating information helps define a person as an individual, rather than as a member of a group or social category.
Theories	Theories are logically self-consistent models or frameworks describing the behavior of a certain natural or social phenomenon. They are broad explanations and predictions concerning phenomena of interest.
Superordinate	Superordinate goal refers to a goal that exceeds or overrides all others; a goal that renders

goal	other goals relatively less important.
Superordinate	A hypernym is a word whose extension includes the extension of the word of which it is a hypernym. A word that is more generic or broad than another given word. Another term for a hypernym is a superordinate.
Chronic	Chronic refers to a relatively long duration, usually more than a few months.
Priming	A phenomenon in which exposure to a word or concept later makes it easier to recall related information, even when one has no conscious memory of the word or concept is called priming.
Social identity theory	Social identity theory formed by Henri Tajfel and John Turner focuses on the psychological basis of intergroup discrimination. It is composed of three elements: Categorization, Identification, and Comparison.
Social identity	Social identity is the way we define ourselves in terms of group membership.
Personal identity	The portion of the self-concept that pertains to the self as a distinct, separate individual is called personal identity.
Negative feedback	In negative feedback, the output of a system is added back into the input, so as to reverse the direction of change. This tends to keep the output from changing, so it is stabilizing and attempts to maintain homeostasis.
Feedback	Feedback refers to information returned to a person about the effects a response has had.
Self-image	A person's self-image is the mental picture, generally of a kind that is quite resistant to change, that depicts not only details that are potentially available to objective investigation by others, but also items that have been learned by that person about himself or herself.
Individual differences	Individual differences psychology studies the ways in which individual people differ in their behavior. This is distinguished from other aspects of psychology in that although psychology is ostensibly a study of individuals, modern psychologists invariably study groups.
Cultural values	The importance and desirability of various objects and activities as defined by people in a given culture are referred to as cultural values.
Collectivist	A person who defines the self in terms of relationships to other people and groups and gives priority to group goals is called collectivist.
Individualist	A person who defines the self in terms of personal traits and gives priority to personal goals is an individualist.
Social role theory	The theory that small gender differences are magnified in perception by the contrasting social roles occupied by men and women is called social role theory.
Role theory	Role theory is a perspective that considers most of everyday activity to be living up to the roles, or expectations, of others. The central weakness of role theory is in describing and explaining deviant behavior.
Social role	Social role refers to expected behavior patterns associated with particular social positions.
Confederate	Someone who is posing as a participant in an experiment but is actually assisting the experimenter is a confederate.
Eating disorders	Psychological disorders characterized by distortion of the body image and gross disturbances in eating patterns are called eating disorders.
Anxiety	Anxiety is a complex combination of the feeling of fear, apprehension and worry often accompanied by physical sensations such as palpitations, chest pain and/or shortness of breath.

Go to **Cram101.com** for the Practice Tests for this Chapter.

Go to **Cram101.com** for the Practice Tests for this Chapter.
And, **NEVER** highlight a book again!

Obsession	An obsession is a thought or idea that the sufferer cannot stop thinking about. Common examples include fears of acquiring disease, getting hurt, or causing harm to someone. They are typically automatic, frequent, distressing, and difficult to control or put an end to by themselves.
Sexual harassment	Deliberate or repeated verbal comments, gestures, or physical contact of a sexual nature that is unwanted by the recipient is called sexual harassment.
Personality	Personality refers to the pattern of enduring characteristics that differentiates a person, the patterns of behaviors that make each individual unique.
Ambivalent sexism	A form of sexism characterized by attitudes about women that reflect both negative, resentful beliefs and feelings and affectionate, chivalrous, but potentially patronizing beliefs and feelings is referred to as ambivalent sexism.
Insight	Insight refers to a sudden awareness of the relationships among various elements that had previously appeared to be independent of one another.
Guilt	Guilt describes many concepts related to a negative emotion or condition caused by actions which are believed to be, morally wrong. According to Freud, the avoidance of guilt is the basis for moral behavior.
Reaction time	The amount of time required to respond to a stimulus is referred to as reaction time.
Empirical evidence	Facts or information based on direct observation or experience are referred to as empirical evidence.
Empirical	Empirical means the use of working hypotheses which are capable of being disproved using observation or experiment.
Contact hypothesis	The contact hypothesis suggests that prejudice can be reduced through increased contact among members of different social groups.
Wisdom	Wisdom is the ability to make correct judgments and decisions. It is an intangible quality gained through experience. Whether or not something is wise is determined in a pragmatic sense by its popularity, how long it has been around, and its ability to predict against future events.
Social norm	A social norm, is a rule that is socially enforced. In social situations, such as meetings, they are unwritten and often unstated rules that govern individuals' behavior. A social norm is most evident when not followed or broken.
Cooperative learning	Cooperative learning was proposed in response to traditional curriculum-driven education. In cooperative learning environments, students interact in purposively structured heterogenous group to support the learning of one self and others in the same group.
Jigsaw classroom	The Jigsaw Classroom experiment compared traditional competitive classroom learning with interdependent cooperative learning. Students in the cooperative jigsaw groups demonstrated lower ethnic discrimination, fewer stereotyped attitudes, and higher academic achivement.
Recategorization	Shifts in the boundary between an individual's in-group and an out-group, causing persons formerly viewed as out-group members to now be viewed as belonging to the in-group are called recategorization.
Questionnaire	A self-report method of data collection or clinical assessment method in which the individual being studied checks off items on a printed list, answers multiple-choice questions, or writes out answers to essay questions aimed at producing a selfdescription is called questionnaire.
Reverse discrimination	Reverse discrimination is a term used to describe discriminatory policies or acts that benefit a historically sociopolitically nondominant group (typically minorities), rather than

	the historically sociopolitically dominant group.
Stereotype threat	A stereotype threat is perceived by persons who believe that they will be evaluated in terms of stereotypes. This is a potential influence on test performance, the resulting anxiety that one's behavior might confirm a negative stereotype about one's group.
Gender difference	A gender difference is a disparity between genders involving quality or quantity. Though some gender differences are controversial, they are not to be confused with sexist stereotypes.
Gender identity	Gender identity describes the gender with which a person identifies, but can also be used to refer to the gender that other people attribute to the individual on the basis of what they know from gender role indications.
Ethnic identity	An enduring, basic aspect of the self that includes a sense of membership in an ethnic group and the attitudes and feelings related to that membership is called an ethnic identity.

Attitude	An enduring mental representation of a person, place, or thing that evokes an emotional response and related behavior is called attitude.
Self-esteem	Self-esteem refers to a person's subjective appraisal of himself or herself as intrinsically positive or negative to some degree.
Prejudice	Prejudice in general, implies coming to a judgment on the subject before learning where the preponderance of the evidence actually lies, or formation of a judgement without direct experience.
Social psychology	Social psychology is the study of the nature and causes of human social behavior, with an emphasis on how people think towards each other and how they relate to each other.
Affect	A subjective feeling or emotional tone often accompanied by bodily expressions noticeable to others is called affect.
Ambivalence	The simultaneous holding of strong positive and negative emotional attitudes toward the same situation or person is called ambivalence.
Emotion	An emotion is a mental states that arise spontaneously, rather than through conscious effort. They are often accompanied by physiological changes.
Reflex	A simple, involuntary response to a stimulus is referred to as reflex. Reflex actions originate at the spinal cord rather than the brain.
Survey	A method of scientific investigation in which a large sample of people answer questions about their attitudes or behavior is referred to as a survey.
Social desirability bias	Social desirability bias is the inclination to present oneself in a manner that will be viewed favourably by others. Being by nature social creatures, all people are inclined to seek some degree of social acceptance, and as with other psychological terms, "social desirability" is by no means an epithet.
Cocaine	Cocaine is a crystalline tropane alkaloid that is obtained from the leaves of the coca plant. It is a stimulant of the central nervous system and an appetite suppressant, creating what has been described as a euphoric sense of happiness and increased energy.
Overt behavior	An action or response that is directly observable and measurable is an overt behavior.
Pupil	In the eye, the pupil is the opening in the middle of the iris. It appears black because most of the light entering it is absorbed by the tissues inside the eye. The size of the pupil is controlled by involuntary contraction and dilation of the iris, in order to regulate the intensity of light entering the eye. This is known as the pupillary reflex.
Facial electromyograph	The facial electromyograph is an electronic instrument that records facial muscle activity associated with emotions and attitudes.
Electromyograph	Electromyography (EMG) is a medical technique for measuring muscle response to nervous stimulation. EMG is performed using an instrument called an electromyograph, to produce a record called an electromyogram. An electromyograph detects the electrical potential generated by muscle cells when these cells contract.
Brain	The brain controls and coordinates most movement, behavior and homeostatic body functions such as heartbeat, blood pressure, fluid balance and body temperature. Functions of the brain are responsible for cognition, emotion, memory, motor learning and other sorts of learning. The brain is primarily made up of two types of cells: glia and neurons.
Stimulus	A change in an environmental condition that elicits a response is a stimulus.
Nightmare	Nightmare was the original term for the state later known as waking dream, and more currently as sleep paralysis, associated with rapid eye movement (REM) periods of sleep.

Go to **Cram101.com** for the Practice Tests for this Chapter.

Discrimination	In Learning theory, discrimination refers the ability to distinguish between a conditioned stimulus and other stimuli. It can be brought about by extensive training or differential reinforcement. In social terms, it is the denial of privileges to a person or a group on the basis of prejudice.
Correlation	A statistical technique for determining the degree of association between two or more variables is referred to as correlation.
Theory of planned behavior	The theory of planned behavior links attitudes and behavior. It holds that human action is guided by three kinds of considerations: Beliefs about the likely outcomes of the behavior and the evaluations of these outcomes; Beliefs about the normative expectations of others and motivation to comply with these expectations; and, Beliefs about the presence of factors that may facilitate or impede performance of the behavior and the perceived power of these factors.
Theories	Theories are logically self-consistent models or frameworks describing the behavior of a certain natural or social phenomenon. They are broad explanations and predictions concerning phenomena of interest.
Norms	In testing, standards of test performance that permit the comparison of one person's score on the test to the scores of others who have taken the same test are referred to as norms.
Hypothesis	A specific statement about behavior or mental processes that is testable through research is a hypothesis.
Identical twins	Identical twins occur when a single egg is fertilized to form one zygote (monozygotic) but the zygote then divides into two separate embryos. The two embryos develop into foetuses sharing the same womb. Monozygotic twins are genetically identical unless there has been a mutation in development, and they are almost always the same gender.
Fraternal twins	Fraternal twins usually occur when two fertilized eggs are implanted in the uterine wall at the same time. The two eggs form two zygotes, and these twins are therefore also known as dizygotic. Dizygotic twins are no more similar genetically than any siblings.
Social norm	A social norm, is a rule that is socially enforced. In social situations, such as meetings, they are unwritten and often unstated rules that govern individuals' behavior. A social norm is most evident when not followed or broken.
Temperament	Temperament refers to a basic, innate disposition to change behavior. The activity level is an important dimension of temperament.
Personality	Personality refers to the pattern of enduring characteristics that differentiates a person, the patterns of behaviors that make each individual unique.
Trait	An enduring personality characteristic that tends to lead to certain behaviors is called a trait. The term trait also means a genetically inherited feature of an organism.
Marijuana	Marijuana is the dried vegetable matter of the Cannabis sativa plant. It contains large concentrations of compounds that have medicinal and psychoactive effects when consumed, usually by smoking or eating.
Ingroup	An ingroup is a social group towards which an individual feels loyalty and respect, usually due to membership in the group. This loyalty often manifests itself as an ingroup bias.
Learning	Learning is a relatively permanent change in behavior that results from experience. Thus, to attribute a behavioral change to learning, the change must be relatively permanent and must result from experience.
Scheme	According to Piaget, a hypothetical mental structure that permits the classification and organization of new information is called a scheme.

Chapter 6. Attitudes

55

Go to **Cram101.com** for the Practice Tests for this Chapter.
And, **NEVER** highlight a book again!

Elaboration	The extensiveness of processing at any given level of memory is called elaboration. The use of elaboration changes developmentally. Adolescents are more likely to use elaboration spontaneously than children.
Heuristic	A heuristic is a simple, efficient rule of thumb proposed to explain how people make decisions, come to judgments and solve problems, typically when facing complex problems or incomplete information. These rules work well under most circumstances, but in certain cases lead to systematic cognitive biases.
Statistics	Statistics is a type of data analysis which practice includes the planning, summarizing, and interpreting of observations of a system possibly followed by predicting or forecasting of future events based on a mathematical model of the system being observed.
Statistic	A statistic is an observable random variable of a sample.
Motivation	In psychology, motivation is the driving force (desire) behind all actions of an organism.
Stereotype	A stereotype is considered to be a group concept, held by one social group about another. They are often used in a negative or prejudicial sense and are frequently used to justify certain discriminatory behaviors. This allows powerful social groups to legitimize and protect their dominant position
Physical attractiveness	Physical attractiveness is the perception of an individual as physically beautiful by other people.
Attention	Attention is the cognitive process of selectively concentrating on one thing while ignoring other things. Psychologists have labeled three types of attention: sustained attention, selective attention, and divided attention.
Primacy effect	The primacy effect is a cognitive bias that results from disproportionate salience of initial stimuli or observations. If, for example, a subject reads a sufficiently-long list of words, he or she is more likely to remember words read toward the beginning than words read in the middle.
Recency effect	Recency effect refers to the tendency to recall the last items in a series of items. The tendency to evaluate others in terms of the most recent impression.
Simulation	A simulation is an imitation of some real device or state of affairs. Simulation attempts to represent certain features of the behavior of a physical or abstract system by the behavior of another system.
Lesbian	A lesbian is a homosexual woman. They are women who are sexually and romantically attracted to other women.
Anxiety	Anxiety is a complex combination of the feeling of fear, apprehension and worry often accompanied by physical sensations such as palpitations, chest pain and/or shortness of breath.
Incentive	An incentive is what is expected once a behavior is performed. An incentive acts as a reinforcer.
Chronic	Chronic refers to a relatively long duration, usually more than a few months.
Subliminal persuasion	Subliminal persuasion refers to sending persuasive messages below the recipient's level of awareness.
Suicide	Suicide behavior is rare in childhood but escalates in adolescence. The suicide rate increases in a linear fashion from adolescence through late adulthood.
Field study	Field study refers to any scientific research study in which data are collected in a setting other than the laboratory.

Go to **Cram101.com** for the Practice Tests for this Chapter.

Insight	Insight refers to a sudden awareness of the relationships among various elements that had previously appeared to be independent of one another.
Individual differences	Individual differences psychology studies the ways in which individual people differ in their behavior. This is distinguished from other aspects of psychology in that although psychology is ostensibly a study of individuals, modern psychologists invariably study groups.
Cognition	The intellectual processes through which information is obtained, transformed, stored, retrieved, and otherwise used is cognition.
Individualism	Individualism refers to putting personal goals ahead of group goals and defining one's identity in terms of personal attributes rather than group memberships.
Collectivism	Collectivism is an emphasis on the group, as opposed to the individual. It is syndrome of attitudes and behaviors based on the belief that the basic unit of survival lies within a group, not the individual.
Individuality	According to Cooper, individuality consists of two dimensions: self-assertion and separateness.
Reactance	Reactance is a negative emotional and cognitive reaction to a restriction of one's freedom that can be associated with various medical regimens or therapies.
Analogy	An analogy is a comparison between two different things, in order to highlight some form of similarity. Analogy is the cognitive process of transferring information from a particular subject to another particular subject.
Psychological reactance	Psychological reactance is a social psychological phenomenon in which pressure to respond in a certain way tends to push the person to behave in the opposite way.
Cognitive dissonance	Cognitive dissonance is a state of opposition between cognitions. Contradicting cognitions serve as a driving force that compel the mind to acquire or invent new thoughts or beliefs, or to modify existing beliefs, so as to minimize the amount of dissonance between cognitions.
Maladaptive	In psychology, a behavior or trait is adaptive when it helps an individual adjust and function well within their social environment. A maladaptive behavior or trait is counterproductive to the individual.
Control group	A group that does not receive the treatment effect in an experiment is referred to as the control group or sometimes as the comparison group.
Confederate	Someone who is posing as a participant in an experiment but is actually assisting the experimenter is a confederate.
Punishment	Punishment is the addtion of a stimulus that reduces the frequency of a response, or the removal of a stimulus that results in a reduction of the response.
Psychotherapy	Psychotherapy is a set of techniques based on psychological principles intended to improve mental health, emotional or behavioral issues.
Effort justification	In cognitive-dissonance theory, the tendency to seek justification for strenuous efforts is called effort justification.
Empirical	Empirical means the use of working hypotheses which are capable of being disproved using observation or experiment.
Impression management	Impression management is the process through which people try to control the impressions other people form of them.
Self-concept	Self-concept refers to domain-specific evaluations of the self where a domain may be academics, athletics, etc.

Go to **Cram101.com** for the Practice Tests for this Chapter.
And, **NEVER** highlight a book again!

Negative feedback	In negative feedback, the output of a system is added back into the input, so as to reverse the direction of change. This tends to keep the output from changing, so it is stabilizing and attempts to maintain homeostasis.
Feedback	Feedback refers to information returned to a person about the effects a response has had.
Personality test	A personality test aims to describe aspects of a person's character that remain stable across situations.
Self-perception theory	Self-perception theory is an account of attitude change developed by Daryl Bem. It asserts that we only have that knowledge of our own behavior and its cauzation that another person can have, and that we develop our attitudes by observing our own behavior and concluding what attitudes must have caused them.

Go to **Cram101.com** for the Practice Tests for this Chapter.

Conformity	Conformity is the degree to which members of a group will change their behavior, views and attitudes to fit the views of the group. The group can influence members via unconscious processes or via overt social pressure on individuals.
Norms	In testing, standards of test performance that permit the comparison of one person's score on the test to the scores of others who have taken the same test are referred to as norms.
Obedience	Obedience is the willingness to follow the will of others. Humans have been shown to be surprisingly obedient in the presence of perceived legitimate authority figures, as demonstrated by the Milgram experiment in the 1960s.
Social influence	Social influence is when the actions or thoughts of individual(s) are changed by other individual(s). Peer pressure is an example of social influence.
Suicide	Suicide behavior is rare in childhood but escalates in adolescence. The suicide rate increases in a linear fashion from adolescence through late adulthood.
Confederate	Someone who is posing as a participant in an experiment but is actually assisting the experimenter is a confederate.
Habit	A habit is a response that has become completely separated from its eliciting stimulus. Early learning theorists used the term to describe S-R associations, however not all S-R associations become a habit, rather many are extinguished after reinforcement is withdrawn.
Individuality	According to Cooper, individuality consists of two dimensions: self-assertion and separateness.
Social norm	A social norm, is a rule that is socially enforced. In social situations, such as meetings, they are unwritten and often unstated rules that govern individuals' behavior. A social norm is most evident when not followed or broken.
Social psychology	Social psychology is the study of the nature and causes of human social behavior, with an emphasis on how people think towards each other and how they relate to each other.
Laboratory study	Any research study in which the subjects are brought to a specially designated area that has been set up to facilitate the researcher's ability to control the environment or collect data is referred to as a laboratory study.
Perception	Perception is the process of acquiring, interpreting, selecting, and organizing sensory information.
Optical illusion	An optical illusion is any illusion that deceives the human visual system into perceiving something that is not present or incorrectly perceiving what is present. There are physiological illusions and cognitive illusions.
Illusion	An illusion is a distortion of a sensory perception.
Affect	A subjective feeling or emotional tone often accompanied by bodily expressions noticeable to others is called affect.
Nerve	A nerve is an enclosed, cable-like bundle of nerve fibers or axons, which includes the glia that ensheath the axons in myelin. Neurons are sometimes called nerve cells, though this term is technically imprecise since many neurons do not form nerves.
Control group	A group that does not receive the treatment effect in an experiment is referred to as the control group or sometimes as the comparison group.
Informational influence	Informational influence is the use of others' behaviors or opinions as information in forming one's own judgment about the objective nature of an event or situation.
Normative influence	The normative influence is the effect on an individual that results from a concern about what others will think of them if they behave in a certain way or express a certain belief.

Go to **Cram101.com** for the Practice Tests for this Chapter.

Normative	The term normative is used to describe the effects of those structures of culture which regulate the function of social activity.
Overt behavior	An action or response that is directly observable and measurable is an overt behavior.
Incentive	An incentive is what is expected once a behavior is performed. An incentive acts as a reinforcer.
Attitude	An enduring mental representation of a person, place, or thing that evokes an emotional response and related behavior is called attitude.
Attention	Attention is the cognitive process of selectively concentrating on one thing while ignoring other things. Psychologists have labeled three types of attention: sustained attention, selective attention, and divided attention.
Individual differences	Individual differences psychology studies the ways in which individual people differ in their behavior. This is distinguished from other aspects of psychology in that although psychology is ostensibly a study of individuals, modern psychologists invariably study groups.
Personality	Personality refers to the pattern of enduring characteristics that differentiates a person, the patterns of behaviors that make each individual unique.
Trait	An enduring personality characteristic that tends to lead to certain behaviors is called a trait. The term trait also means a genetically inherited feature of an organism.
Stages	Stages represent relatively discrete periods of time in which functioning is qualitatively different from functioning at other periods.
Adolescence	The period of life bounded by puberty and the assumption of adult responsibilities is adolescence.
Gender difference	A gender difference is a disparity between genders involving quality or quantity. Though some gender differences are controversial, they are not to be confused with sexist stereotypes.
Autonomy	Autonomy is the condition of something that does not depend on anything else.
Hypothesis	A specific statement about behavior or mental processes that is testable through research is a hypothesis.
Interdependence	Interdependence is a dynamic of being mutually responsible to and dependent on others.
Individualism	Individualism refers to putting personal goals ahead of group goals and defining one's identity in terms of personal attributes rather than group memberships.
Meta-analysis	In statistics, a meta-analysis combines the results of several studies that address a set of related research hypotheses.
Theories	Theories are logically self-consistent models or frameworks describing the behavior of a certain natural or social phenomenon. They are broad explanations and predictions concerning phenomena of interest.
Reciprocity	Reciprocity, in interpersonal attraction, is the tendency to return feelings and attitudes that are expressed about us.
Reciprocity norm	The rule that people should pay back in kind what they receive from others is called the reciprocity norm.
Questionnaire	A self-report method of data collection or clinical assessment method in which the individual being studied checks off items on a printed list, answers multiple-choice questions, or writes out answers to essay questions aimed at producing a selfdescription is called questionnaire.
Wisdom	Wisdom is the ability to make correct judgments and decisions. It is an intangible quality

Go to **Cram101.com** for the Practice Tests for this Chapter.

gained through experience. Whether or not something is wise is determined in a pragmatic sense by its popularity, how long it has been around, and its ability to predict against future events.

Foot-in-the-door	The tendency for a person who has first complied with a small request to be more likely later to fulfill a larger request is called the foot-in-the-door effect.
Self-image	A person's self-image is the mental picture, generally of a kind that is quite resistant to change, that depicts not only details that are potentially available to objective investigation by others, but also items that have been learned by that person about himself or herself.
Reflection	Reflection is the process of rephrasing or repeating thoughts and feelings expressed, making the person more aware of what they are saying or thinking.
Door-in-the-face	A strategy in which someone makes a large, unreasonable request with the expectation that the person will refuse but will then be more likely to respond favorably to a smaller request at a later time is called the door-in-the-face technique.
Psychological reactance	Psychological reactance is a social psychological phenomenon in which pressure to respond in a certain way tends to push the person to behave in the opposite way.
Reactance	Reactance is a negative emotional and cognitive reaction to a restriction of one's freedom that can be associated with various medical regimens or therapies.
Homosexual	Homosexual refers to a sexual orientation characterized by aesthetic attraction, romantic love, and sexual desire exclusively for members of the same sex or gender identity.
Punishment	Punishment is the addtion of a stimulus that reduces the frequency of a response, or the removal of a stimulus that results in a reduction of the response.
Learning	Learning is a relatively permanent change in behavior that results from experience. Thus, to attribute a behavioral change to learning, the change must be relatively permanent and must result from experience.
Psychiatrist	A psychiatrist is a physician who specializes in the diagnosis and treatment of psychological disorders.
Baseline	Measure of a particular behavior or process taken before the introduction of the independent variable or treatment is called the baseline.
Prejudice	Prejudice in general, implies coming to a judgment on the subject before learning where the preponderance of the evidence actually lies, or formation of a judgement without direct experience.
Field study	Field study refers to any scientific research study in which data are collected in a setting other than the laboratory.
Paradigm	Paradigm refers to the set of practices that defines a scientific discipline during a particular period of time. It provides a framework from which to conduct research, it ensures that a certain range of phenomena, those on which the paradigm focuses, are explored thoroughly. Itmay also blind scientists to other, perhaps more fruitful, ways of dealing with their subject matter.
Script	A schema, or behavioral sequence, for an event is called a script. It is a form of schematic organization, with real-world events organized in terms of temporal and causal relations between component acts.
Correlation	A statistical technique for determining the degree of association between two or more variables is referred to as correlation.

Go to **Cram101.com** for the Practice Tests for this Chapter.
And, **NEVER** highlight a book again!

Human nature	Human nature is the fundamental nature and substance of humans, as well as the range of human behavior that is believed to be invariant over long periods of time and across very different cultural contexts.
Physical proximity	Physical proximity refers to one's actual physical nearness to others in terms of housing, work, school, and so forth.
Free will	The idea that human beings are capable of freely making choices or decisions is free will.

Social influence	Social influence is when the actions or thoughts of individual(s) are changed by other individual(s). Peer pressure is an example of social influence.
Attitude	An enduring mental representation of a person, place, or thing that evokes an emotional response and related behavior is called attitude.
Stereotype	A stereotype is considered to be a group concept, held by one social group about another. They are often used in a negative or prejudicial sense and are frequently used to justify certain discriminatory behaviors. This allows powerful social groups to legitimize and protect their dominant position
Affect	A subjective feeling or emotional tone often accompanied by bodily expressions noticeable to others is called affect.
Social psychology	Social psychology is the study of the nature and causes of human social behavior, with an emphasis on how people think towards each other and how they relate to each other.
Theories	Theories are logically self-consistent models or frameworks describing the behavior of a certain natural or social phenomenon. They are broad explanations and predictions concerning phenomena of interest.
Hypothesis	A specific statement about behavior or mental processes that is testable through research is a hypothesis.
Instinct	Instinct is the word used to describe inherent dispositions towards particular actions. They are generally an inherited pattern of responses or reactions to certain kinds of situations.
Evolution	Commonly used to refer to gradual change, evolution is the change in the frequency of alleles within a population from one generation to the next. This change may be caused by different mechanisms, including natural selection, genetic drift, or changes in population (gene flow).
Species	Species refers to a reproductively isolated breeding population.
Stimulus	A change in an environmental condition that elicits a response is a stimulus.
Learning	Learning is a relatively permanent change in behavior that results from experience. Thus, to attribute a behavioral change to learning, the change must be relatively permanent and must result from experience.
Social facilitation	Social facilitation refers to the process by which a person's performance is increased when other members of a group engage in similar behavior.
Meta-analysis	In statistics, a meta-analysis combines the results of several studies that address a set of related research hypotheses.
Perception	Perception is the process of acquiring, interpreting, selecting, and organizing sensory information.
Attention	Attention is the cognitive process of selectively concentrating on one thing while ignoring other things. Psychologists have labeled three types of attention: sustained attention, selective attention, and divided attention.
Social loafing	Social loafing is the phenomenon that persons make less effort to achieve a goal when they work in a group than when they work alone. This is one of the main reasons that groups sometimes perform less than the combined performance of their members working as individuals.
Collectivist	A person who defines the self in terms of relationships to other people and groups and gives priority to group goals is called collectivist.
Individualist	A person who defines the self in terms of personal traits and gives priority to personal goals is an individualist.

Go to **Cram101.com** for the Practice Tests for this Chapter.

Collective effort model	The collective effort model is an explanation of social loafing. Perceived links between individuals' efforts and their outcomes are weaker when they work together. The result is a tendency toward social loafing.
Anxiety	Anxiety is a complex combination of the feeling of fear, apprehension and worry often accompanied by physical sensations such as palpitations, chest pain and/or shortness of breath.
Rape	Rape is a crime where the victim is forced into sexual activity, in particular sexual penetration, against his or her will.
Population	Population refers to all members of a well-defined group of organisms, events, or things.
Deindividuation	Deindividuation refers to the phenomenon of relinquishing one's sense of identity. This can happen as a result of becoming part of a group.
Individuality	According to Cooper, individuality consists of two dimensions: self-assertion and separateness.
Self-awareness	Realization that one's existence and functioning are separate from those of other people and things is called self-awareness.
Consciousness	The awareness of the sensations, thoughts, and feelings being experienced at a given moment is called consciousness.
Suicide	Suicide behavior is rare in childhood but escalates in adolescence. The suicide rate increases in a linear fashion from adolescence through late adulthood.
Personal identity	The portion of the self-concept that pertains to the self as a distinct, separate individual is called personal identity.
Confederate	Someone who is posing as a participant in an experiment but is actually assisting the experimenter is a confederate.
Social identity	Social identity is the way we define ourselves in terms of group membership.
Norms	In testing, standards of test performance that permit the comparison of one person's score on the test to the scores of others who have taken the same test are referred to as norms.
Conformity	Conformity is the degree to which members of a group will change their behavior, views and attitudes to fit the views of the group. The group can influence members via unconscious processes or via overt social pressure on individuals.
Prejudice	Prejudice in general, implies coming to a judgment on the subject before learning where the preponderance of the evidence actually lies, or formation of a judgement without direct experience.
Social identity theory	Social identity theory formed by Henri Tajfel and John Turner focuses on the psychological basis of intergroup discrimination. It is composed of three elements: Categorization, Identification, and Comparison.
Socialization	Social rules and social relations are created, communicated, and changed in verbal and nonverbal ways creating social complexity useful in identifying outsiders and intelligent breeding partners. The process of learning these skills is called socialization.
Stages	Stages represent relatively discrete periods of time in which functioning is qualitatively different from functioning at other periods.
Cohesiveness	Cohesiveness with respect to conformity is the degree of attraction felt by an individual toward an influencing group.
Feedback	Feedback refers to information returned to a person about the effects a response has had.

Go to **Cram101.com** for the Practice Tests for this Chapter.

Positive relationship	Statistically, a positive relationship refers to a mathematical relationship in which increases in one measure are matched by increases in the other.
Interdependence	Interdependence is a dynamic of being mutually responsible to and dependent on others.
Risky shift	The risky shift occurs when the group collectively agrees on a course of action that is likewise more extreme than they would have made if asked individually. Risky shift is one side of a more general phenomenon called group polarization.
Polarization	Polarization is the process of preparing a neuron for firing by creating an internal negative charge in relation to the body fluid outside the cell membrane.
Group polarization	The solidification and further strengthening of a position as a consequence of a group discussion is called a group polarization effect.
Questionnaire	A self-report method of data collection or clinical assessment method in which the individual being studied checks off items on a printed list, answers multiple-choice questions, or writes out answers to essay questions aimed at producing a selfdescription is called questionnaire.
Reasoning	Reasoning is the act of using reason to derive a conclusion from certain premises. There are two main methods to reach a conclusion,deductive reasoning and inductive reasoning.
Social comparison	Social comparison theory is the idea that individuals learn about and assess themselves by comparison with other people. Research shows that individuals tend to lean more toward social comparisons in situations that are ambiguous.
Social categorization	Social categorization refers to the tendency to divide the social world into two separate categories: one's in-group and various out-groups.
Ingroup	An ingroup is a social group towards which an individual feels loyalty and respect, usually due to membership in the group. This loyalty often manifests itself as an ingroup bias.
Launching	The process in which youths move into adulthood and exit their family of origin is called launching. It can be a time to formulate life goals, to develop an identity, and to become more independent before joining with another person to form a new family.
Groupthink	In a groupthink situation, each member of the group attempts to conform his or her opinions to what they believe to be the consensus of the group.
Motivation	In psychology, motivation is the driving force (desire) behind all actions of an organism.
Illusion	An illusion is a distortion of a sensory perception.
Wisdom	Wisdom is the ability to make correct judgments and decisions. It is an intangible quality gained through experience. Whether or not something is wise is determined in a pragmatic sense by its popularity, how long it has been around, and its ability to predict against future events.
Group cohesiveness	The strength of the liking relationships linking group members to each other and to the group itself is referred to as group cohesiveness.
Empirical	Empirical means the use of working hypotheses which are capable of being disproved using observation or experiment.
Variable	A variable refers to a measurable factor, characteristic, or attribute of an individual or a system.
Information processing	Information processing is an approach to the goal of understanding human thinking. The essence of the approach is to see cognition as being essentially computational in nature, with mind being the software and the brain being the hardware.

Go to **Cram101.com** for the Practice Tests for this Chapter.

Antecedents	In behavior modification, events that typically precede the target response are called antecedents.
Additive task	Additive task is when a group's performance is the sum of all the individual members' performances.
Process loss	Time spent by group members that is not devoted to task accomplishment is called process loss.
Brainstorming	Brainstorming is an organized approach for producing ideas by letting the mind think without interruption. The term was coined by Alex Osborn.
Creativity	Creativity is the ability to think about something in novel and unusual ways and come up with unique solutions to problems. It involves divergent thinking, having many solutions or views to a problem.
Heuristic	A heuristic is a simple, efficient rule of thumb proposed to explain how people make decisions, come to judgments and solve problems, typically when facing complex problems or incomplete information. These rules work well under most circumstances, but in certain cases lead to systematic cognitive biases.
Projection	Attributing one's own undesirable thoughts, impulses, traits, or behaviors to others is referred to as projection.
Ethnicity	Ethnicity refers to a characteristic based on cultural heritage, nationality characteristics, race, religion, and language.
Clique	A clique is an informal and restricted social group formed by a number of people who share common. Social roles vary, but two roles commonly associated with a female clique is notably applicable to most - that of the "queen bee" and that of the "outcast".
Motives	Needs or desires that energize and direct behavior toward a goal are motives.
Social dilemma	Social dilemma refers to a situation in which a particular action will benefit the individual who takes it, harm the individuals who don't, and cause more harm than benefit to everyone if everyone takes it.
Paradigm	Paradigm refers to the set of practices that defines a scientific discipline during a particular period of time. It provides a framework from which to conduct research, it ensures that a certain range of phenomena, those on which the paradigm focuses, are explored thoroughly. Itmay also blind scientists to other, perhaps more fruitful, ways of dealing with their subject matter.
Reciprocity	Reciprocity, in interpersonal attraction, is the tendency to return feelings and attitudes that are expressed about us.
Conditioning	Conditioning describes the process by which behaviors can be learned or modified through interaction with the environment.
Superordinate goal	Superordinate goal refers to a goal that exceeds or overrides all others; a goal that renders other goals relatively less important.
Superordinate	A hypernym is a word whose extension includes the extension of the word of which it is a hypernym. A word that is more generic or broad than another given word. Another term for a hypernym is a superordinate.
Syndrome	The term syndrome is the association of several clinically recognizable features, signs, symptoms, phenomena or characteristics which often occur together, so that the presence of one feature indicates the presence of the others.
Empathy	Empathy is the recognition and understanding of the states of mind, including beliefs,

Go to **Cram101.com** for the Practice Tests for this Chapter.

desires and particularly emotions of others without injecting your own.

Go to **Cram101.com** for the Practice Tests for this Chapter.

Attachment	Attachment is the tendency to seek closeness to another person and feel secure when that person is present.
Anxiety	Anxiety is a complex combination of the feeling of fear, apprehension and worry often accompanied by physical sensations such as palpitations, chest pain and/or shortness of breath.
Social anxiety	A feeling of apprehension in the presence of others is social anxiety.
Nightmare	Nightmare was the original term for the state later known as waking dream, and more currently as sleep paralysis, associated with rapid eye movement (REM) periods of sleep.
Motivation	In psychology, motivation is the driving force (desire) behind all actions of an organism.
Need for Affiliation	Need for Affiliation is a term introduced by David McClelland to describe a person's need to feel like he needs to belong to a group. These individuals require warm interpersonal relationships and approval from those in these relationships is very satisfying. People who value affiliation a lot tend to be good team members, but poor leaders.
Species	Species refers to a reproductively isolated breeding population.
Attention	Attention is the cognitive process of selectively concentrating on one thing while ignoring other things. Psychologists have labeled three types of attention: sustained attention, selective attention, and divided attention.
Laboratory setting	Research setting in which the behavior of interest does not naturally occur is called a laboratory setting.
Shyness	A tendency to avoid others plus uneasiness and strain when socializing is called shyness.
Personality trait	According to the Diagnostic and Statistical Manual of the American Psychiatric Association, a personality trait is a "prominent aspect of personality that is exhibited in a wide range of important social and personal contexts. ...".
Personality	Personality refers to the pattern of enduring characteristics that differentiates a person, the patterns of behaviors that make each individual unique.
Trait	An enduring personality characteristic that tends to lead to certain behaviors is called a trait. The term trait also means a genetically inherited feature of an organism.
Longitudinal research	Research that studies the same subjects over an extended period of time, usually several years or more, is called longitudinal research.
Temperament	Temperament refers to a basic, innate disposition to change behavior. The activity level is an important dimension of temperament.
Emotion	An emotion is a mental states that arise spontaneously, rather than through conscious effort. They are often accompanied by physiological changes.
Friendship	The essentials of friendship are reciprocity and commitment between individuals who see themselves more or less as equals. Interaction between friends rests on a more equal power base than the interaction between children and adults.
Evolutionary psychology	Evolutionary psychology proposes that cognition and behavior can be better understood in light of evolutionary history.
Evolution	Commonly used to refer to gradual change, evolution is the change in the frequency of alleles within a population from one generation to the next. This change may be caused by different mechanisms, including natural selection, genetic drift, or changes in population (gene flow).
Homosexual	Homosexual refers to a sexual orientation characterized by aesthetic attraction, romantic love, and sexual desire exclusively for members of the same sex or gender identity.

Go to **Cram101.com** for the Practice Tests for this Chapter.
And, **NEVER** highlight a book again!

Population	Population refers to all members of a well-defined group of organisms, events, or things.
Affect	A subjective feeling or emotional tone often accompanied by bodily expressions noticeable to others is called affect.
Lesbian	A lesbian is a homosexual woman. They are women who are sexually and romantically attracted to other women.
Physical proximity	Physical proximity refers to one's actual physical nearness to others in terms of housing, work, school, and so forth.
Wisdom	Wisdom is the ability to make correct judgments and decisions. It is an intangible quality gained through experience. Whether or not something is wise is determined in a pragmatic sense by its popularity, how long it has been around, and its ability to predict against future events.
Stimulus	A change in an environmental condition that elicits a response is a stimulus.
Physical attractiveness	Physical attractiveness is the perception of an individual as physically beautiful by other people.
Statistics	Statistics is a type of data analysis which practice includes the planning, summarizing, and interpreting of observations of a system possibly followed by predicting or forecasting of future events based on a mathematical model of the system being observed.
Statistic	A statistic is an observable random variable of a sample.
Hypothesis	A specific statement about behavior or mental processes that is testable through research is a hypothesis.
Perception	Perception is the process of acquiring, interpreting, selecting, and organizing sensory information.
Contrast effect	A contrast effect is the enhancement or diminishment, relative to normal, of a perception and related performance as a result of immediately previous or simultaneous exposure to a stimulus of lesser or greater value in the same dimension.
Stereotype	A stereotype is considered to be a group concept, held by one social group about another. They are often used in a negative or prejudicial sense and are frequently used to justify certain discriminatory behaviors. This allows powerful social groups to legitimize and protect their dominant position
Social skills	Social skills are skills used to interact and communicate with others to assist status in the social structure and other motivations.
Self-esteem	Self-esteem refers to a person's subjective appraisal of himself or herself as intrinsically positive or negative to some degree.
Collectivist	A person who defines the self in terms of relationships to other people and groups and gives priority to group goals is called collectivist.
Interpersonal attraction	Interpersonal attraction is the attraction between people which leads to friendships and romantic relationships. Major variables include propinquity, similarity, familiarity, reciprocal liking, and physical attractiveness.
Feedback	Feedback refers to information returned to a person about the effects a response has had.
Obsession	An obsession is a thought or idea that the sufferer cannot stop thinking about. Common examples include fears of acquiring disease, getting hurt, or causing harm to someone. They are typically automatic, frequent, distressing, and difficult to control or put an end to by themselves.

Go to **Cram101.com** for the Practice Tests for this Chapter.
And, **NEVER** highlight a book again!

Eating disorders	Psychological disorders characterized by distortion of the body image and gross disturbances in eating patterns are called eating disorders.
Bulimia	Bulimia refers to a disorder in which a person binges on incredibly large quantities of food, then purges by vomiting or by using laxatives. Bulimia is often less about food, and more to do with deep psychological issues and profound feelings of lack of control.
Anorexia nervosa	Anorexia nervosa is an eating disorder characterized by voluntary starvation and exercise stress.
Mania	Mania is a medical condition characterized by severely elevated mood. Mania is most usually associated with bipolar disorder, where episodes of mania may cyclically alternate with episodes of depression.
Stages	Stages represent relatively discrete periods of time in which functioning is qualitatively different from functioning at other periods.
Attitude	An enduring mental representation of a person, place, or thing that evokes an emotional response and related behavior is called attitude.
Survey	A method of scientific investigation in which a large sample of people answer questions about their attitudes or behavior is referred to as a survey.
Random selection	Choosing a sample so that each member of the population has an equal chance of being included in the sample is called random selection.
Variable	A variable refers to a measurable factor, characteristic, or attribute of an individual or a system.
Reciprocity	Reciprocity, in interpersonal attraction, is the tendency to return feelings and attitudes that are expressed about us.
Confederate	Someone who is posing as a participant in an experiment but is actually assisting the experimenter is a confederate.
Psychological reactance	Psychological reactance is a social psychological phenomenon in which pressure to respond in a certain way tends to push the person to behave in the opposite way.
Reactance	Reactance is a negative emotional and cognitive reaction to a restriction of one's freedom that can be associated with various medical regimens or therapies.
Correlation	A statistical technique for determining the degree of association between two or more variables is referred to as correlation.
Motives	Needs or desires that energize and direct behavior toward a goal are motives.
Evolutionary perspective	A perspective that focuses on how humans have evolved and adapted behaviors required for survival against various environmental pressures over the long course is called the evolutionary perspective.
Interdependence	Interdependence is a dynamic of being mutually responsible to and dependent on others.
Stage theory	Stage theory characterizes development by hypothesizing the existence of distinct, and often critical, periods of life. Each period follows one another in an orderly sequence.
Script	A schema, or behavioral sequence, for an event is called a script. It is a form of schematic organization, with real-world events organized in terms of temporal and causal relations between component acts.
Theories	Theories are logically self-consistent models or frameworks describing the behavior of a certain natural or social phenomenon. They are broad explanations and predictions concerning phenomena of interest.

Go to **Cram101.com** for the Practice Tests for this Chapter.

Social exchange theory	Social exchange theory explains social change and stability as a process of negotiated exchanges between parties. Social exchange theory posits that all human relationships are formed by the use of a subjective cost-benefit analysis and the comparison of alternatives.
Exchange theory	A relationship in which the participants expect and desire strict reciprocity in their interactions is referred to as exchange theory.
Equity theory	Equity theory suggests that people are most satisfied with a relationship when the ratio between benefits and contributions is similar.
Compensation	In personaility, compensation, according to Adler, is an effort to overcome imagined or real inferiorities by developing one's abilities.
Communal relationship	A relationship in which the participants expect and provide mutual responsiveness to each other's needs is a communal relationship.
Child development	Scientific study of the processes of change from conception through adolescence is called child development.
Psychiatrist	A psychiatrist is a physician who specializes in the diagnosis and treatment of psychological disorders.
Secure attachment style	In Bartholomew's model, a secure attachment style is characterized by high self-esteem and high interpersonal trust. It is usually described as the ideal and most successful attachment style.
Secure attachment	With secure attachment, the infant uses a caregiver as a secure base from which to explore the environment. Ainsworth believes that secure attachment in the first year of life provides an important foundation for psychological development later in life.
Attachment style	Attachment style refers to the way a person typically interacts with significant others.
Romantic love	An intense, positive emotion that involves sexual attraction, feelings of caring, and the belief that one is in love is romantic love.
Insecure-avoidant attachment	An anxious emotional bond marked by a tendency to avoid reunion with a parent or caregiver is called insecure-avoidant attachment.
Avoidant attachment	A type of insecure attachment characterized by apparent indifference to the leave-takings of, and reunions with, an attachment figure is referred to as avoidant attachment.
Prognosis	A forecast about the probable course of an illess is referred to as prognosis.
Infancy	The developmental period that extends from birth to 18 or 24 months is called infancy.
Scheme	According to Piaget, a hypothetical mental structure that permits the classification and organization of new information is called a scheme.
Passionate love	A state of intense absorption includes intense physiological arousal, psychological interest, and caring for the needs of another is referred to as passionate love.
Companionate love	Companionate love is a form of love that combines friendship and commitment. Companionate love is generally a personal relation you build with somebody you share your life with, but with no sexual or physical desire.
Excitation transfer	The process whereby arousal caused by one stimulus is added to arousal from a second stimulus and the combined arousal is attributed to the second stimulus is called excitation transfer.
Field study	Field study refers to any scientific research study in which data are collected in a setting other than the laboratory.
Questionnaire	A self-report method of data collection or clinical assessment method in which the individual

Go to **Cram101.com** for the Practice Tests for this Chapter.

being studied checks off items on a printed list, answers multiple-choice questions, or writes out answers to essay questions aimed at producing a selfdescription is called questionnaire.

Individualism	Individualism refers to putting personal goals ahead of group goals and defining one's identity in terms of personal attributes rather than group memberships.
Stimulant	A stimulant is a drug which increases the activity of the sympathetic nervous system and produces a sense of euphoria or awakeness.
Self-disclosure	The process of revealing private thoughts, feelings, and one's personal history to others is referred to as self-disclosure.
Meta-analysis	In statistics, a meta-analysis combines the results of several studies that address a set of related research hypotheses.
Psychoanalytic theory	Psychoanalytic theory is a general term for approaches to psychoanalysis which attempt to provide a conceptual framework more-or-less independent of clinical practice rather than based on empirical analysis of clinical cases.
Psychoanalytic	Freud's theory that unconscious forces act as determinants of personality is called psychoanalytic theory. The theory is a developmental theory characterized by critical stages of development.
Variability	Statistically, variability refers to how much the scores in a distribution spread out, away from the mean.
Brain	The brain controls and coordinates most movement, behavior and homeostatic body functions such as heartbeat, blood pressure, fluid balance and body temperature. Functions of the brain are responsible for cognition, emotion, memory, motor learning and other sorts of learning. The brain is primarily made up of two types of cells: glia and neurons.

Passive compliance	Effortlessly bending to unreasonable demands or circumstances is called passive compliance.
Evolution	Commonly used to refer to gradual change, evolution is the change in the frequency of alleles within a population from one generation to the next. This change may be caused by different mechanisms, including natural selection, genetic drift, or changes in population (gene flow).
Evolutionary perspective	A perspective that focuses on how humans have evolved and adapted behaviors required for survival against various environmental pressures over the long course is called the evolutionary perspective.
Gene	A gene is an ultramicroscopic area of the chromosome. It is the smallest physical unit of the DNA molecule that carries a piece of hereditary information.
Species	Species refers to a reproductively isolated breeding population.
Learning	Learning is a relatively permanent change in behavior that results from experience. Thus, to attribute a behavioral change to learning, the change must be relatively permanent and must result from experience.
Kin selection	Kin selection has been mathematically defined by Hamilton as a mechanism for the evolution of apparently altruistic acts. Under natural selection, a gene that causes itself to increase in frequency should become more common in the population. Since identical copies of genes may be carried in relatives, a gene in one organism that prompts behavior which aids another organism carrying the same gene may become more successful.
Reciprocity	Reciprocity, in interpersonal attraction, is the tendency to return feelings and attitudes that are expressed about us.
Altruism	Altruism is being helpful to other people with little or no interest in being rewarded for one's efforts. This is distinct from merely helping others.
Field experiment	A field experiment applies the scientific method to experimentally examine an intervention in the real world rather than in the laboratory. Field experiments generally randomize subjects into treatment and control groups and compare outcomes between these groups.
Natural selection	Natural selection is a process by which biological populations are altered over time, as a result of the propagation of heritable traits that affect the capacity of individual organisms to survive and reproduce.
Ingroup	An ingroup is a social group towards which an individual feels loyalty and respect, usually due to membership in the group. This loyalty often manifests itself as an ingroup bias.
Empirical evidence	Facts or information based on direct observation or experience are referred to as empirical evidence.
Empirical	Empirical means the use of working hypotheses which are capable of being disproved using observation or experiment.
Self-esteem	Self-esteem refers to a person's subjective appraisal of himself or herself as intrinsically positive or negative to some degree.
Multiple sclerosis	Multiple sclerosis affects neurons, the cells of the brain and spinal cord that carry information, create thought and perception, and allow the brain to control the body. Surrounding and protecting these neurons is a layer of fat, called myelin, which helps neurons carry electrical signals. MS causes gradual destruction of myelin (demyelination) in patches throughout the brain and/or spinal cord, causing various symptoms depending upon which signals are interrupted.
Self-awareness	Realization that one's existence and functioning are separate from those of other people and things is called self-awareness.

Go to **Cram101.com** for the Practice Tests for this Chapter.

Adolescence	The period of life bounded by puberty and the assumption of adult responsibilities is adolescence.
Discrimination	In Learning theory, discrimination refers the ability to distinguish between a conditioned stimulus and other stimuli. It can be brought about by extensive training or differential reinforcement. In social terms, it is the denial of privileges to a person or a group on the basis of prejudice.
Hypocrisy	Publicly advocating some attitude or behavior and then acting in a way that is inconsistent with this espoused attitude or behavior is called hypocrisy.
Motivation	In psychology, motivation is the driving force (desire) behind all actions of an organism.
Attention	Attention is the cognitive process of selectively concentrating on one thing while ignoring other things. Psychologists have labeled three types of attention: sustained attention, selective attention, and divided attention.
Toddler	A toddler is a child between the ages of one and three years old. During this period, the child learns a great deal about social roles and develops motor skills; to toddle is to walk unsteadily.
Hypothesis	A specific statement about behavior or mental processes that is testable through research is a hypothesis.
Rape	Rape is a crime where the victim is forced into sexual activity, in particular sexual penetration, against his or her will.
Conformity	Conformity is the degree to which members of a group will change their behavior, views and attitudes to fit the views of the group. The group can influence members via unconscious processes or via overt social pressure on individuals.
Norms	In testing, standards of test performance that permit the comparison of one person's score on the test to the scores of others who have taken the same test are referred to as norms.
Theories	Theories are logically self-consistent models or frameworks describing the behavior of a certain natural or social phenomenon. They are broad explanations and predictions concerning phenomena of interest.
Motives	Needs or desires that energize and direct behavior toward a goal are motives.
Empathy	Empathy is the recognition and understanding of the states of mind, including beliefs, desires and particularly emotions of others without injecting your own.
Perspective taking	Perspective taking refers to the ability to assume another person's perspective and understand his or her thoughts and feelings. An adolescent can step outside a two-person interchange and view the interaction from a third-person perspective; younger children cannot.
Empathy-altruism hypothesis	The empathy-altruism hypothesis suggests that prosocial behavior is motivated solely by the desire to help someone in need.
Random assignment	Assignment of participants to experimental and control groups by chance is called random assignment. Random assigment reduces the likelihood that the results are due to preexisiting systematic differences between the groups.
Confederate	Someone who is posing as a participant in an experiment but is actually assisting the experimenter is a confederate.
Guilt	Guilt describes many concepts related to a negative emotion or condition caused by actions which are believed to be, morally wrong. According to Freud, the avoidance of guilt is the

Go to **Cram101.com** for the Practice Tests for this Chapter.

basis for moral behavior.

Semantics	Semantics is a subfield of linguistics that is traditionally defined as the study of meaning of words, phrases, sentences, and texts.
Egoism	Egoism is the view that we are always motivated by self-interest, even in seeming acts of altruism.
Survey	A method of scientific investigation in which a large sample of people answer questions about their attitudes or behavior is referred to as a survey.
Homosexual	Homosexual refers to a sexual orientation characterized by aesthetic attraction, romantic love, and sexual desire exclusively for members of the same sex or gender identity.
Emotion	An emotion is a mental states that arise spontaneously, rather than through conscious effort. They are often accompanied by physiological changes.
Human nature	Human nature is the fundamental nature and substance of humans, as well as the range of human behavior that is believed to be invariant over long periods of time and across very different cultural contexts.
Social norm	A social norm, is a rule that is socially enforced. In social situations, such as meetings, they are unwritten and often unstated rules that govern individuals' behavior. A social norm is most evident when not followed or broken.
Bystander effect	Bystander effect refers to individuals who observe an emergency help less when someone else is present than when they are alone.
Stimulus	A change in an environmental condition that elicits a response is a stimulus.
Affect	A subjective feeling or emotional tone often accompanied by bodily expressions noticeable to others is called affect.
Pluralistic ignorance	Pluralistic ignorance is involves several members of a group who think that they have different perceptions, beliefs, or attitudes from the rest of the group. While they do not endorse the group norm, the dissenting persons behave like the other group members, because they think that the behavior of the other group members shows that the opinion of the group is unanimous.
Wisdom	Wisdom is the ability to make correct judgments and decisions. It is an intangible quality gained through experience. Whether or not something is wise is determined in a pragmatic sense by its popularity, how long it has been around, and its ability to predict against future events.
Questionnaire	A self-report method of data collection or clinical assessment method in which the individual being studied checks off items on a printed list, answers multiple-choice questions, or writes out answers to essay questions aimed at producing a selfdescription is called questionnaire.
Diffusion of responsibility	Diffusion of responsibility is a social phenomenon which tends to occur in groups of people above a certain critical size when responsibility is not explicitly assigned.
Suicide	Suicide behavior is rare in childhood but escalates in adolescence. The suicide rate increases in a linear fashion from adolescence through late adulthood.
Audience inhibition	Audience inhibition is the reluctance to act for fear of making an uncertain impression on observers.
Population	Population refers to all members of a well-defined group of organisms, events, or things.
Social psychology	Social psychology is the study of the nature and causes of human social behavior, with an emphasis on how people think towards each other and how they relate to each other.

Go to **Cram101.com** for the Practice Tests for this Chapter.

Variable	A variable refers to a measurable factor, characteristic, or attribute of an individual or a system.
Depression	In everyday language depression refers to any downturn in mood, which may be relatively transitory and perhaps due to something trivial. This is differentiated from Clinical depression which is marked by symptoms that last two weeks or more and are so severe that they interfere with daily living.
Modeling	A type of behavior learned through observation of others demonstrating the same behavior is modeling.
Stereotype	A stereotype is considered to be a group concept, held by one social group about another. They are often used in a negative or prejudicial sense and are frequently used to justify certain discriminatory behaviors. This allows powerful social groups to legitimize and protect their dominant position
Prejudice	Prejudice in general, implies coming to a judgment on the subject before learning where the preponderance of the evidence actually lies, or formation of a judgement without direct experience.
Friendship	The essentials of friendship are reciprocity and commitment between individuals who see themselves more or less as equals. Interaction between friends rests on a more equal power base than the interaction between children and adults.
Attitude	An enduring mental representation of a person, place, or thing that evokes an emotional response and related behavior is called attitude.
Individual differences	Individual differences psychology studies the ways in which individual people differ in their behavior. This is distinguished from other aspects of psychology in that although psychology is ostensibly a study of individuals, modern psychologists invariably study groups.
Personality	Personality refers to the pattern of enduring characteristics that differentiates a person, the patterns of behaviors that make each individual unique.
Trait	An enduring personality characteristic that tends to lead to certain behaviors is called a trait. The term trait also means a genetically inherited feature of an organism.
Longitudinal study	Longitudinal study is a type of developmental study in which the same group of participants is followed and measured for an extended period of time, often years.
Early adulthood	The developmental period beginning in the late teens or early twenties and lasting into the thirties is called early adulthood; characterized by an increasing self-awareness.
Collectivist	A person who defines the self in terms of relationships to other people and groups and gives priority to group goals is called collectivist.
Individualist	A person who defines the self in terms of personal traits and gives priority to personal goals is an individualist.
Extroversion	Extroversion refers to the tendency to be outgoing, adaptable, and sociable.
Agreeableness	Agreeableness, one of the big-five personality traits, reflects individual differences in concern with cooperation and social harmony. It is the degree individuals value getting along with others.
Insight	Insight refers to a sudden awareness of the relationships among various elements that had previously appeared to be independent of one another.
Reasoning	Reasoning is the act of using reason to derive a conclusion from certain premises. There are two main methods to reach a conclusion, deductive reasoning and inductive reasoning.
Baseline	Measure of a particular behavior or process taken before the introduction of the independent

Go to **Cram101.com** for the Practice Tests for this Chapter.

variable or treatment is called the baseline.

Alcoholic	An alcoholic is dependent on alcohol as characterized by craving, loss of control, physical dependence and withdrawal symptoms, and tolerance.
Communal relationship	A relationship in which the participants expect and provide mutual responsiveness to each other's needs is a communal relationship.
Exchange relationship	A relationship in which the participants expect and desire strict reciprocity in their interactions is referred to as an exchange relationship.
Ego	In Freud's view the Ego serves to balance our primitive needs and our moral beliefs and taboos. Relying on experience, a healthy Ego provides the ability to adapt to reality and interact with the outside world.
Social support	Social Support is the physical and emotional comfort given by family, friends, co-workers and others. Research has identified three main types of social support: emotional, practical, sharing points of view.
Threat-to-self-esteem model	Threat-to-self-esteem model suggests that reactions to the receiving of assistance depends on whether help is perceived as supportive or threatening.
Work motivation	The conditions and processes responsible for the arousal, direction, magnitude, and maintenance of effort one puts forth in one's job is called the work motivation.
Scheme	According to Piaget, a hypothetical mental structure that permits the classification and organization of new information is called a scheme.

Theories	Theories are logically self-consistent models or frameworks describing the behavior of a certain natural or social phenomenon. They are broad explanations and predictions concerning phenomena of interest.
Attention	Attention is the cognitive process of selectively concentrating on one thing while ignoring other things. Psychologists have labeled three types of attention: sustained attention, selective attention, and divided attention.
Statistic	A statistic is an observable random variable of a sample.
Statistics	Statistics is a type of data analysis which practice includes the planning, summarizing, and interpreting of observations of a system possibly followed by predicting or forecasting of future events based on a mathematical model of the system being observed.
Chronic	Chronic refers to a relatively long duration, usually more than a few months.
Depression	In everyday language depression refers to any downturn in mood, which may be relatively transitory and perhaps due to something trivial. This is differentiated from Clinical depression which is marked by symptoms that last two weeks or more and are so severe that they interfere with daily living.
Self-esteem	Self-esteem refers to a person's subjective appraisal of himself or herself as intrinsically positive or negative to some degree.
Emotion	An emotion is a mental states that arise spontaneously, rather than through conscious effort. They are often accompanied by physiological changes.
Attitude	An enduring mental representation of a person, place, or thing that evokes an emotional response and related behavior is called attitude.
Emotional aggression	Emotional aggression refers to inflicting harm for its own sake.
Genitals	Genitals refers to the internal and external reproductive organs.
Population	Population refers to all members of a well-defined group of organisms, events, or things.
Cocaine	Cocaine is a crystalline tropane alkaloid that is obtained from the leaves of the coca plant. It is a stimulant of the central nervous system and an appetite suppressant, creating what has been described as a euphoric sense of happiness and increased energy.
Stereotype	A stereotype is considered to be a group concept, held by one social group about another.They are often used in a negative or prejudicial sense and are frequently used to justify certain discriminatory behaviors. This allows powerful social groups to legitimize and protect their dominant position
Relational aggression	Relational Aggression usually stems from miscommunication and the unsynchronisation of feelings between the partners. The unspoken tension between partners in this kind of problematic relationship tends to manifest itself in aggression towards the partner in subtle, but potentially devastating mannerisms.
Overt aggression	Aggression that is openly directed at its target is referred to as overt aggression.
Meta-analysis	In statistics, a meta-analysis combines the results of several studies that address a set of related research hypotheses.
Gender difference	A gender difference is a disparity between genders involving quality or quantity. Though some gender differences are controversial, they are not to be confused with sexist stereotypes.
Learning	Learning is a relatively permanent change in behavior that results from experience. Thus, to attribute a behavioral change to learning, the change must be relatively permanent and must result from experience.

Instinct	Instinct is the word used to describe inherent dispositions towards particular actions. They are generally an inherited pattern of responses or reactions to certain kinds of situations.
Evolutionary psychology	Evolutionary psychology proposes that cognition and behavior can be better understood in light of evolutionary history.
Gene	A gene is an ultramicroscopic area of the chromosome. It is the smallest physical unit of the DNA molecule that carries a piece of hereditary information.
Hormone	A hormone is a chemical messenger from one cell (or group of cells) to another. The best known are those produced by endocrine glands, but they are produced by nearly every organ system. The function of hormones is to serve as a signal to the target cells; the action of the hormone is determined by the pattern of secretion and the signal transduction of the receiving tissue.
Neurotransmitter	A neurotransmitter is a chemical that is used to relay, amplify and modulate electrical signals between a neurons and another cell.
Psychoanalysis	Psychoanalysis refers to the school of psychology that emphasizes the importance of unconscious motives and conflicts as determinants of human behavior. It was Freud's method of exploring human personality.
Motivation	In psychology, motivation is the driving force (desire) behind all actions of an organism.
Natural selection	Natural selection is a process by which biological populations are altered over time, as a result of the propagation of heritable traits that affect the capacity of individual organisms to survive and reproduce.
Scientific research	Research that is objective, systematic, and testable is called scientific research.
Reasoning	Reasoning is the act of using reason to derive a conclusion from certain premises. There are two main methods to reach a conclusion,deductive reasoning and inductive reasoning.
Instinct theory	The notion that human behavior is motivated by certain innate tendencies, or instincts, shared by all individuals is an instinct theory.
Evolution	Commonly used to refer to gradual change, evolution is the change in the frequency of alleles within a population from one generation to the next. This change may be caused by different mechanisms, including natural selection, genetic drift, or changes in population (gene flow).
Evolutionary perspective	A perspective that focuses on how humans have evolved and adapted behaviors required for survival against various environmental pressures over the long course is called the evolutionary perspective.
Species	Species refers to a reproductively isolated breeding population.
Hypothesis	A specific statement about behavior or mental processes that is testable through research is a hypothesis.
Genetics	Genetics is the science of genes, heredity, and the variation of organisms.
Personality	Personality refers to the pattern of enduring characteristics that differentiates a person, the patterns of behaviors that make each individual unique.
Personality type	A persistent style of complex behaviors defined by a group of related traits is referred to as a personality type. Myer Friedman and his co-workers first defined personality types in the 1950s. Friedman classified people into 2 categories, Type A and Type B.
Heritability	Heritability It is that proportion of the observed variation in a particular phenotype within a particular population, that can be attributed to the contribution of genotype. In other words: it measures the extent to which differences between individuals in a population are

due their being different genetically.

Monozygotic	Identical twins occur when a single egg is fertilized to form one zygote, calld monozygotic, but the zygote then divides into two separate embryos. The two embryos develop into foetuses sharing the same womb. Monozygotic twins are genetically identical unless there has been a mutation in development, and they are almost always the same gender.
Dizygotic	Fraternal twins (commonly known as "non-identical twins") usually occur when two fertilized eggs are implanted in the uterine wall at the same time. The two eggs form two zygotes, and these twins are therefore also known as dizygotic.
Trait	An enduring personality characteristic that tends to lead to certain behaviors is called a trait. The term trait also means a genetically inherited feature of an organism.
Testosterone	Testosterone is a steroid hormone from the androgen group. It is the principal male sex hormone and the "original" anabolic steroid.
Alzheimer's disease	Alzheimer's disease is an incurable, degenerative neuropsychiatric disease which results in a pervasive loss of first mental, then physical functioning due to the deterioration of brain tissue.
Positive correlation	A relationship between two variables in which both vary in the same direction is called a positive correlation.
Correlation	A statistical technique for determining the degree of association between two or more variables is referred to as correlation.
Socioeconomic Status	A family's socioeconomic status is based on family income, parental education level, parental occupation, and social status in the community. Those with high status often have more success in preparing their children for school because they have access to a wide range of resources.
Socioeconomic	Socioeconomic pertains to the study of the social and economic impacts of any product or service offering, market intervention or other activity on an economy as a whole and on the companies, organization and individuals who are its main economic actors.
Deprivation	Deprivation, is the loss or withholding of normal stimulation, nutrition, comfort, love, and so forth; a condition of lacking. The level of stimulation is less than what is required.
Serotonin	Serotonin, a neurotransmitter, is believed to play an important part of the biochemistry of depression, bipolar disorder and anxiety. It is also believed to be influential on sexuality and appetite.
Nervous system	The body's electrochemical communication circuitry, made up of billions of neurons is a nervous system.
Positive reinforcement	In positive reinforcement, a stimulus is added and the rate of responding increases.
Reinforcement	In operant conditioning, reinforcement is any change in an environment that (a) occurs after the behavior, (b) seems to make that behavior re-occur more often in the future and (c) that reoccurence of behavior must be the result of the change.
Negative reinforcement	During negative reinforcement, a stimulus is removed and the frequency of the behavior or response increases.
Punishment	Punishment is the addtion of a stimulus that reduces the frequency of a response, or the removal of a stimulus that results in a reduction of the response.
Corporal punishment	Corporal punishment is the use of physical force with the intention of causing pain, but not injury.

Go to **Cram101.com** for the Practice Tests for this Chapter.

Positive relationship	Statistically, a positive relationship refers to a mathematical relationship in which increases in one measure are matched by increases in the other.
Random assignment	Assignment of participants to experimental and control groups by chance is called random assignment. Random assigment reduces the likelihood that the results are due to preexisiting systematic differences between the groups.
Social learning theory	Social learning theory explains the process of gender typing in terms of observation, imitation, and role playing .
Social learning	Social learning is learning that occurs as a function of observing, retaining and replicating behavior observed in others. Although social learning can occur at any stage in life, it is thought to be particularly important during childhood, particularly as authority becomes important.
Affect	A subjective feeling or emotional tone often accompanied by bodily expressions noticeable to others is called affect.
Construct	A generalized concept, such as anxiety or gravity, is a construct.
Script	A schema, or behavioral sequence, for an event is called a script. It is a form of schematic organization, with real-world events organized in terms of temporal and causal relations between component acts.
Social role	Social role refers to expected behavior patterns associated with particular social positions.
Confederate	Someone who is posing as a participant in an experiment but is actually assisting the experimenter is a confederate.
Norms	In testing, standards of test performance that permit the comparison of one person's score on the test to the scores of others who have taken the same test are referred to as norms.
Nurture	Nurture refers to the environmental influences on behavior due to nutrition, culture, socioeconomic status, and learning.
Information processing	Information processing is an approach to the goal of understanding human thinking. The essence of the approach is to see cognition as being essentially computational in nature, with mind being the software and the brain being the hardware.
Physiological drives	Unlearned drives with a biological basis, such as hunger, thirst, and avoidance of pain are called physiological drives. Physiological drives are homeostatic where action is directed to return the organsim to a state of equlibrium.
Displacement	An unconscious defense mechanism in which the individual directs aggressive or sexual feelings away from the primary object to someone or something safe is referred to as displacement. Displacement in linguistics is simply the ability to talk about things not present.
Catharsis	Catharsis has been adopted by modern psychotherapy as the act of giving expression to deep emotions often associated with events in the individuals past which have never before been adequately expressed.
Clique	A clique is an informal and restricted social group formed by a number of people who share common. Social roles vary, but two roles commonly associated with a female clique is notably applicable to most - that of the "queen bee" and that of the "outcast".
Negative correlation	A negative correlation refers to a relationship between two variables in which one variable increases as the other decreases.
Validity	The extent to which a test measures what it is intended to measure is called validity.
Empirical	Facts or information based on direct observation or experience are referred to as empirical

evidence	evidence.
Empirical	Empirical means the use of working hypotheses which are capable of being disproved using observation or experiment.
Displaced aggression	Redirecting aggression to a target other than the actual source of one's frustration is a defense mechanism called displaced aggression.
Excitation transfer	The process whereby arousal caused by one stimulus is added to arousal from a second stimulus and the combined arousal is attributed to the second stimulus is called excitation transfer.
Stimulus	A change in an environmental condition that elicits a response is a stimulus.
Arousal-affect model	The arousal-affect model proposes that aggression is influenced by both the intensity of arousal and the type of emotion produced by a stimulus.
Cognition	The intellectual processes through which information is obtained, transformed, stored, retrieved, and otherwise used is cognition.
Perception	Perception is the process of acquiring, interpreting, selecting, and organizing sensory information.
Motives	Needs or desires that energize and direct behavior toward a goal are motives.
Anxiety	Anxiety is a complex combination of the feeling of fear, apprehension and worry often accompanied by physical sensations such as palpitations, chest pain and/or shortness of breath.
Alcohol myopia	Alcohol myopia refers to condition in which a person under the influence of alcohol ignores the long-range consequences of his or her behavior and responds only to the poorly thought-out immediate aspects of a situation.
Myopia	Myopia is a refractive defect of the eye in which light focuses in front of the retina. Those with myopia are often described as nearsighted or short-sighted in that they typically can see nearby objects clearly but distant objects appear blurred because the lens cannot flatten enough.
Variable	A variable refers to a measurable factor, characteristic, or attribute of an individual or a system.
Empathy	Empathy is the recognition and understanding of the states of mind, including beliefs, desires and particularly emotions of others without injecting your own.
Habituation	In habituation there is a progressive reduction in the response probability with continued repetition of a stimulus.
Rape	Rape is a crime where the victim is forced into sexual activity, in particular sexual penetration, against his or her will.
Social isolation	Social isolation refers to a type of loneliness that occurs when a person lacks a sense of integrated involvement. Being deprived of participation in a group or community involving companionship, shared interests, organized activities, and meaningful roles causes a person to feel alone.
Survey	A method of scientific investigation in which a large sample of people answer questions about their attitudes or behavior is referred to as a survey.
Sexual abuse	Sexual abuse is a term used to describe non- consensual sexual relations between two or more parties which are considered criminally and/or morally offensive.
Substance abuse	Substance abuse refers to the overindulgence in and dependence on a stimulant, depressant, or other chemical substance, leading to effects that are detrimental to the individual's

physical or mental health, or the welfare of others.

Social support	Social Support is the physical and emotional comfort given by family, friends, co-workers and others. Research has identified three main types of social support: emotional, practical, sharing points of view.
Modeling	A type of behavior learned through observation of others demonstrating the same behavior is modeling.
Socialization	Social rules and social relations are created, communicated, and changed in verbal and nonverbal ways creating social complexity useful in identifying outsiders and intelligent breeding partners. The process of learning these skills is called socialization.
Debriefing	Process of informing a participant after the experiment about the nature of the experiment, clarifying any misunderstanding, and answering any questions that the participant may have concerning the experiment is called debriefing.
Launching	The process in which youths move into adulthood and exit their family of origin is called launching. It can be a time to formulate life goals, to develop an identity, and to become more independent before joining with another person to form a new family.

Chapter 11. Aggression

Attention	Attention is the cognitive process of selectively concentrating on one thing while ignoring other things. Psychologists have labeled three types of attention: sustained attention, selective attention, and divided attention.
Social psychology	Social psychology is the study of the nature and causes of human social behavior, with an emphasis on how people think towards each other and how they relate to each other.
Stages	Stages represent relatively discrete periods of time in which functioning is qualitatively different from functioning at other periods.
Representative sample	Representative sample refers to a sample of participants selected from the larger population in such a way that important subgroups within the population are included in the sample in the same proportions as they are found in the larger population.
Personality	Personality refers to the pattern of enduring characteristics that differentiates a person, the patterns of behaviors that make each individual unique.
Theories	Theories are logically self-consistent models or frameworks describing the behavior of a certain natural or social phenomenon. They are broad explanations and predictions concerning phenomena of interest.
Stereotype	A stereotype is considered to be a group concept, held by one social group about another. They are often used in a negative or prejudicial sense and are frequently used to justify certain discriminatory behaviors. This allows powerful social groups to legitimize and protect their dominant position
Wisdom	Wisdom is the ability to make correct judgments and decisions. It is an intangible quality gained through experience. Whether or not something is wise is determined in a pragmatic sense by its popularity, how long it has been around, and its ability to predict against future events.
Attitude	An enduring mental representation of a person, place, or thing that evokes an emotional response and related behavior is called attitude.
Survey	A method of scientific investigation in which a large sample of people answer questions about their attitudes or behavior is referred to as a survey.
Authoritarian	The term authoritarian is used to describe a style that enforces strong and sometimes oppressive measures against those in its sphere of influence, generally without attempts at gaining their consent.
Individual differences	Individual differences psychology studies the ways in which individual people differ in their behavior. This is distinguished from other aspects of psychology in that although psychology is ostensibly a study of individuals, modern psychologists invariably study groups.
Rape	Rape is a crime where the victim is forced into sexual activity, in particular sexual penetration, against his or her will.
Hypothesis	A specific statement about behavior or mental processes that is testable through research is a hypothesis.
Leniency bias	A general tendency to make favorable assumptions about a person accused of a crime and to favor a verdict of not guilty is referred to as leniency bias.
Variable	A variable refers to a measurable factor, characteristic, or attribute of an individual or a system.
Prejudice	Prejudice in general, implies coming to a judgment on the subject before learning where the preponderance of the evidence actually lies, or formation of a judgement without direct experience.

Go to **Cram101.com** for the Practice Tests for this Chapter.

Punishment	Punishment is the addtion of a stimulus that reduces the frequency of a response, or the removal of a stimulus that results in a reduction of the response.
Intuition	Quick, impulsive thought that does not make use of formal logic or clear reasoning is referred to as intuition.
Guilt	Guilt describes many concepts related to a negative emotion or condition caused by actions which are believed to be, morally wrong. According to Freud, the avoidance of guilt is the basis for moral behavior.
Social isolation	Social isolation refers to a type of loneliness that occurs when a person lacks a sense of integrated involvement. Being deprived of participation in a group or community involving companionship, shared interests, organized activities, and meaningful roles causes a person to feel alone.
Script	A schema, or behavioral sequence, for an event is called a script. It is a form of schematic organization, with real-world events organized in terms of temporal and causal relations between component acts.
Social influence	Social influence is when the actions or thoughts of individual(s) are changed by other individual(s). Peer pressure is an example of social influence.
Internalization	The developmental change from behavior that is externally controlled to behavior that is controlled by internal standards and principles is referred to as internalization.
Confederate	Someone who is posing as a participant in an experiment but is actually assisting the experimenter is a confederate.
Situational attribution	Situational attribution refers to an assumption that a person's behavior is determined by external circumstances such as social pressure.
Attribution theory	Attribution theory is concerned with the ways in which people explain the behavior of others. It explores how individuals "attribute" causes to events and how this cognitive perception affects their motivation.
Fundamental attribution error	The fundamental attribution error is the tendency for people to over-emphasize dispositional, or personality-based, explanations for behaviors observed in others while under-emphasizing the role and power of situational influences on the same behavior.
Polygraph	A polygraph is a device which measures and records several physiological variables such as blood pressure, heart rate, respiration and skin conductivity while a series of questions is being asked, in an attempt to detect lies.
Baseline	Measure of a particular behavior or process taken before the introduction of the independent variable or treatment is called the baseline.
Control questions	In a polygraph exam, questions that almost always provoke anxiety are called control questions.
Brain	The brain controls and coordinates most movement, behavior and homeostatic body functions such as heartbeat, blood pressure, fluid balance and body temperature. Functions of the brain are responsible for cognition, emotion, memory, motor learning and other sorts of learning. The brain is primarily made up of two types of cells: glia and neurons.
Pupil	In the eye, the pupil is the opening in the middle of the iris. It appears black because most of the light entering it is absorbed by the tissues inside the eye. The size of the pupil is controlled by involuntary contraction and dilation of the iris, in order to regulate the intensity of light entering the eye. This is known as the pupillary reflex.
Construct	A generalized concept, such as anxiety or gravity, is a construct.

Go to **Cram101.com** for the Practice Tests for this Chapter.

Semen	Semen is a fluid that contains spermatozoa. It is secreted by the gonads of males for the fertilization of female ova.
Compensation	In personaility, compensation, according to Adler, is an effort to overcome imagined or real inferiorities by developing one's abilities.
Acquisition	Acquisition is the process of adapting to the environment, learning or becoming conditioned. In classical conditoning terms, it is the initial learning of the stimulus response link, which involves a neutral stimulus being associated with a unconditioned stimulus and becoming a conditioned stimulus.
Retrieval	Retrieval is the location of stored information and its subsequent return to consciousness. It is the third stage of information processing.
Alcoholic	An alcoholic is dependent on alcohol as characterized by craving, loss of control, physical dependence and withdrawal symptoms, and tolerance.
Field study	Field study refers to any scientific research study in which data are collected in a setting other than the laboratory.
Ethnic group	An ethnic group is a culture or subculture whose members are readily distinguishable by outsiders based on traits originating from a common racial, national, linguistic, or religious source. Members of an ethnic group are often presumed to be culturally or biologically similar, although this is not in fact necessarily the case.
Sexual harassment	Deliberate or repeated verbal comments, gestures, or physical contact of a sexual nature that is unwanted by the recipient is called sexual harassment.
Genitals	Genitals refers to the internal and external reproductive organs.
Affect	A subjective feeling or emotional tone often accompanied by bodily expressions noticeable to others is called affect.
Feedback	Feedback refers to information returned to a person about the effects a response has had.
Perception	Perception is the process of acquiring, interpreting, selecting, and organizing sensory information.
Consciousness	The awareness of the sensations, thoughts, and feelings being experienced at a given moment is called consciousness.
Reactance	Reactance is a negative emotional and cognitive reaction to a restriction of one's freedom that can be associated with various medical regimens or therapies.
Control group	A group that does not receive the treatment effect in an experiment is referred to as the control group or sometimes as the comparison group.
Euthanasia	Euthanasia is the practice of killing a person or animal, in a painless or minimally painful way, for merciful reasons, usually to end their suffering.
Suicide	Suicide behavior is rare in childhood but escalates in adolescence. The suicide rate increases in a linear fashion from adolescence through late adulthood.
Conformity	Conformity is the degree to which members of a group will change their behavior, views and attitudes to fit the views of the group. The group can influence members via unconscious processes or via overt social pressure on individuals.
Informational influence	Informational influence is the use of others' behaviors or opinions as information in forming one's own judgment about the objective nature of an event or situation.
Normative influence	The normative influence is the effect on an individual that results from a concern about what others will think of them if they behave in a certain way or express a certain belief.

Go to **Cram101.com** for the Practice Tests for this Chapter.

Normative	The term normative is used to describe the effects of those structures of culture which regulate the function of social activity.
Overt behavior	An action or response that is directly observable and measurable is an overt behavior.
Meta-analysis	In statistics, a meta-analysis combines the results of several studies that address a set of related research hypotheses.
Population	Population refers to all members of a well-defined group of organisms, events, or things.
Depression	In everyday language depression refers to any downturn in mood, which may be relatively transitory and perhaps due to something trivial. This is differentiated from Clinical depression which is marked by symptoms that last two weeks or more and are so severe that they interfere with daily living.
Debriefing	Process of informing a participant after the experiment about the nature of the experiment, clarifying any misunderstanding, and answering any questions that the participant may have concerning the experiment is called debriefing.
Procedural justice	Procedural justice concerns the fairness of the processes by which decisions are made.
Inquisitorial model	A dispute-resolution system in which a neutral investigator gathers evidence from both sides and presents the findings in court is referred to as inquisitorial model.
Simulation	A simulation is an imitation of some real device or state of affairs. Simulation attempts to represent certain features of the behavior of a physical or abstract system by the behavior of another system.

Go to **Cram101.com** for the Practice Tests for this Chapter.

Hawthorne effect	The Hawthorne effect refers to improvements in productivity or quality which result not so much because of intended changes to working conditions, but mainly because the workers are aware of extra attention being paid to them.
Affect	A subjective feeling or emotional tone often accompanied by bodily expressions noticeable to others is called affect.
Motivation	In psychology, motivation is the driving force (desire) behind all actions of an organism.
Sexual harassment	Deliberate or repeated verbal comments, gestures, or physical contact of a sexual nature that is unwanted by the recipient is called sexual harassment.
Standardized test	An oral or written assessment for which an individual receives a score indicating how the individual reponded relative to a previously tested large sample of others is referred to as a standardized test.
Personality	Personality refers to the pattern of enduring characteristics that differentiates a person, the patterns of behaviors that make each individual unique.
Trait	An enduring personality characteristic that tends to lead to certain behaviors is called a trait. The term trait also means a genetically inherited feature of an organism.
Social perception	A subfield of social psychology that studies the ways in which we form and modify impressions of others is social perception.
Perception	Perception is the process of acquiring, interpreting, selecting, and organizing sensory information.
Discrimination	In Learning theory, discrimination refers the ability to distinguish between a conditioned stimulus and other stimuli. It can be brought about by extensive training or differential reinforcement. In social terms, it is the denial of privileges to a person or a group on the basis of prejudice.
Social skills	Social skills are skills used to interact and communicate with others to assist status in the social structure and other motivations.
Physical attractiveness	Physical attractiveness is the perception of an individual as physically beautiful by other people.
Modeling	A type of behavior learned through observation of others demonstrating the same behavior is modeling.
Validity	The extent to which a test measures what it is intended to measure is called validity.
Field study	Field study refers to any scientific research study in which data are collected in a setting other than the laboratory.
Self-fulfilling prophecy	A self-fulfilling prophecy is a prediction that, in being made, actually causes itself to become true.
Variable	A variable refers to a measurable factor, characteristic, or attribute of an individual or a system.
Graphology	Graphology is the study of handwriting and its connection to behavior, and related data points. Critics cite the lack of supporting empirical evidence as a reason to not use it. Supporters point to the anecdotal evidence of thousands of positive testimonials, as a reason to use it.
Polygraph	A polygraph is a device which measures and records several physiological variables such as blood pressure, heart rate, respiration and skin conductivity while a series of questions is being asked, in an attempt to detect lies.

Go to **Cram101.com** for the Practice Tests for this Chapter.

Conscientiou-ness	Conscientiousness is one of the dimensions of the five-factor model of personality and individual differences involving being organized, thorough, and reliable as opposed to careless, negligent, and unreliable.
Self-esteem	Self-esteem refers to a person's subjective appraisal of himself or herself as intrinsically positive or negative to some degree.
Personality test	A personality test aims to describe aspects of a person's character that remain stable across situations.
Meta-analysis	In statistics, a meta-analysis combines the results of several studies that address a set of related research hypotheses.
Structured interview	Structured interview refers to an interview in which the questions are set out in a prescribed fashion for the interviewer. It assists professionals in making diagnostic decisions based upon standardized criteria.
Role-playing	Role-playing refers to a technique that teaches people to behave in a certain way by encouraging them to pretend that they are in a particular situation; it helps people acquire complex behaviors in an efficient way.
Reverse discrimination	Reverse discrimination is a term used to describe discriminatory policies or acts that benefit a historically sociopolitically nondominant group (typically minorities), rather than the historically sociopolitically dominant group.
Interdependence	Interdependence is a dynamic of being mutually responsible to and dependent on others.
Feedback	Feedback refers to information returned to a person about the effects a response has had.
Halo effect	The halo effect occurs when a person's positive or negative traits seem to "spill over" from one area of their personality to another in others' perceptions of them.
Creativity	Creativity is the ability to think about something in novel and unusual ways and come up with unique solutions to problems. It involves divergent thinking, having many solutions or views to a problem.
Theories	Theories are logically self-consistent models or frameworks describing the behavior of a certain natural or social phenomenon. They are broad explanations and predictions concerning phenomena of interest.
Contrast effect	A contrast effect is the enhancement or diminishment, relative to normal, of a perception and related performance as a result of immediately previous or simultaneous exposure to a stimulus of lesser or greater value in the same dimension.
Emotion	An emotion is a mental states that arise spontaneously, rather than through conscious effort. They are often accompanied by physiological changes.
Social influence	Social influence is when the actions or thoughts of individual(s) are changed by other individual(s). Peer pressure is an example of social influence.
Great person theory	The great person theory is a view of leadership suggesting that great leaders possess certain traits that set them apart from most human beings, traits that are possessed by all such leaders no matter when or where they lived is called .
Need for Power	Need for Power is a term introduced by David McClelland referring to an individual's need to be in charge. There are two kinds of power, social and personal.
Need for achievement	Need for Achievement is a term introduced by David McClelland into the field of psychology, referring to an individual's desire for significant accomplishment, mastering of skills, control, or high standards.
Reliability	Reliability means the extent to which a test produces a consistent , reproducible score .

Go to **Cram101.com** for the Practice Tests for this Chapter.

Consciousness	The awareness of the sensations, thoughts, and feelings being experienced at a given moment is called consciousness.
Questionnaire	A self-report method of data collection or clinical assessment method in which the individual being studied checks off items on a printed list, answers multiple-choice questions, or writes out answers to essay questions aimed at producing a selfdescription is called questionnaire.
Authoritarian	The term authoritarian is used to describe a style that enforces strong and sometimes oppressive measures against those in its sphere of influence, generally without attempts at gaining their consent.
Stereotype	A stereotype is considered to be a group concept, held by one social group about another.They are often used in a negative or prejudicial sense and are frequently used to justify certain discriminatory behaviors. This allows powerful social groups to legitimize and protect their dominant position
Survey	A method of scientific investigation in which a large sample of people answer questions about their attitudes or behavior is referred to as a survey.
Mentoring	Mentoring refers to a developmental relationship between a more experienced individual and a less experienced partner sometimes referred to as a protégé. In well-designed formal mentoring programs, there are program goals, schedules, and training.
Motives	Needs or desires that energize and direct behavior toward a goal are motives.
Compensation	In personaility, compensation, according to Adler, is an effort to overcome imagined or real inferiorities by developing one's abilities.
Expectancy theory	According to the expectancy theory the amount of effort people exert on a specific task depends on their expectations of the outcome.
Extrinsic motivation	Responding to external incentives such as rewards and punishments is form of extrinsic motivation. Traditionally, extrinsic motivation has been used to motivate employees: Payments, rewards, control, or punishments.
Intrinsic motivation	Intrinsic motivation causes people to engage in an activity for its own sake. They are subjective factors and include self-determination, curiosity, challenge, effort, and others.
Incentive	An incentive is what is expected once a behavior is performed. An incentive acts as a reinforcer.
Equity theory	Equity theory suggests that people are most satisfied with a relationship when the ratio between benefits and contributions is similar.
Statistics	Statistics is a type of data analysis which practice includes the planning, summarizing, and interpreting of observations of a system possibly followed by predicting or forecasting of future events based on a mathematical model of the system being observed.
Statistic	A statistic is an observable random variable of a sample.
Conformity	Conformity is the degree to which members of a group will change their behavior, views and attitudes to fit the views of the group. The group can influence members via unconscious processes or via overt social pressure on individuals.
Social comparison	Social comparison theory is the idea that individuals learn about and assess themselves by comparison with other people. Research shows that individuals tend to lean more toward social comparisons in situations that are ambiguous.
Wisdom	Wisdom is the ability to make correct judgments and decisions. It is an intangible quality gained through experience. Whether or not something is wise is determined in a pragmatic

Go to **Cram101.com** for the Practice Tests for this Chapter.

sense by its popularity, how long it has been around, and its ability to predict against future events.

Hypothesis	A specific statement about behavior or mental processes that is testable through research is a hypothesis.
Simulation	A simulation is an imitation of some real device or state of affairs. Simulation attempts to represent certain features of the behavior of a physical or abstract system by the behavior of another system.
Sunk cost principle	The economic rule of thumb that only future costs and benefits, not past commitments, should be considered in making a decision is the sunk cost principle.

Go to **Cram101.com** for the Practice Tests for this Chapter.

Flooding	Flooding is a behavioral fear-reduction technique based on principles of classical conditioning. Fear-evoking stimuli are presented continuously in the absence of harm so that fear responses are extinguished. However, subjects tend to avoid the stimulus, making extinction difficult.
Anxiety	Anxiety is a complex combination of the feeling of fear, apprehension and worry often accompanied by physical sensations such as palpitations, chest pain and/or shortness of breath.
Phobia	A persistent, irrational fear of an object, situation, or activity that the person feels compelled to avoid is referred to as a phobia.
Depression	In everyday language depression refers to any downturn in mood, which may be relatively transitory and perhaps due to something trivial. This is differentiated from Clinical depression which is marked by symptoms that last two weeks or more and are so severe that they interfere with daily living.
Suicide	Suicide behavior is rare in childhood but escalates in adolescence. The suicide rate increases in a linear fashion from adolescence through late adulthood.
Emotion	An emotion is a mental states that arise spontaneously, rather than through conscious effort. They are often accompanied by physiological changes.
Stress disorder	A significant emotional disturbance caused by stresses outside the range of normal human experience is referred to as stress disorder.
Nightmare	Nightmare was the original term for the state later known as waking dream, and more currently as sleep paralysis, associated with rapid eye movement (REM) periods of sleep.
Attention	Attention is the cognitive process of selectively concentrating on one thing while ignoring other things. Psychologists have labeled three types of attention: sustained attention, selective attention, and divided attention.
Survey	A method of scientific investigation in which a large sample of people answer questions about their attitudes or behavior is referred to as a survey.
Clinical psychologist	A psychologist, usually with a Ph.D, whose training is in the diagnosis, treatment, or research of psychological and behavioral disorders is a clinical psychologist.
Population	Population refers to all members of a well-defined group of organisms, events, or things.
Hypothesis	A specific statement about behavior or mental processes that is testable through research is a hypothesis.
Social readjustment rating scale	Holmes and Rahe's social readjustment rating scale ranks 43 life events from most to least stressful and assigns a point value to each.
Affect	A subjective feeling or emotional tone often accompanied by bodily expressions noticeable to others is called affect.
Motivation	In psychology, motivation is the driving force (desire) behind all actions of an organism.
Deprivation	Deprivation, is the loss or withholding of normal stimulation, nutrition, comfort, love, and so forth; a condition of lacking. The level of stimulation is less than what is required.
Adrenal glands	The adrenal glands sit atop the kidneys. They are chiefly responsible for regulating the stress response through the synthesis of corticosteroids and catecholamines, including cortisol and adrenalin.
Gland	A gland is an organ in an animal's body that synthesizes a substance for release such as hormones, often into the bloodstream or into cavities inside the body or its outer surface.

General adaptation syndrome	The predictable sequence of reactions that organisms show in response to stressors is called the general adaptation syndrome.
Adaptation	Adaptation is a lowering of sensitivity to a stimulus following prolonged exposure to that stimulus. Behavioral adaptations are special ways a particular organism behaves to survive in its natural habitat.
Syndrome	The term syndrome is the association of several clinically recognizable features, signs, symptoms, phenomena or characteristics which often occur together, so that the presence of one feature indicates the presence of the others.
Alarm reaction	The first stage of the general adaptation syndrome, which is triggered by the impact of a stressor and characterized by sympathetic activity is called the alarm reaction.
Adrenaline	Adrenaline refers to a hormone produced by the adrenal medulla that stimulates sympathetic ANS activity and generally arouses people and heightens their emotional responsiveness.
Hormone	A hormone is a chemical messenger from one cell (or group of cells) to another. The best known are those produced by endocrine glands, but they are produced by nearly every organ system. The function of hormones is to serve as a signal to the target cells; the action of the hormone is determined by the pattern of secretion and the signal transduction of the receiving tissue.
Immune system	The most important function of the human immune system occurs at the cellular level of the blood and tissues. The lymphatic and blood circulation systems are highways for specialized white blood cells. These cells include B cells, T cells, natural killer cells, and macrophages. All function with the primary objective of recognizing, attacking and destroying bacteria, viruses, cancer cells, and all substances seen as foreign.
Resistance stage	The resistance stage is the second stage of the general adaptation syndrome. It is characterized by prolonged sympathetic activity in an effort to restore lost energy and repair damage.
Stress hormones	Group of hormones including cortico steroids, that are involved in the body's physiological stress response are referred to as stress hormones.
Exhaustion stage	The third stage of the general adaptation syndrome, characterized by weakened resistance and possible deterioration is referred to as the exhaustion stage.
Evolution	Commonly used to refer to gradual change, evolution is the change in the frequency of alleles within a population from one generation to the next. This change may be caused by different mechanisms, including natural selection, genetic drift, or changes in population (gene flow).
Nervous system	The body's electrochemical communication circuitry, made up of billions of neurons is a nervous system.
Sympathetic	The sympathetic nervous system activates what is often termed the "fight or flight response". It is an automatic regulation system, that is, one that operates without the intervention of conscious thought.
Brain	The brain controls and coordinates most movement, behavior and homeostatic body functions such as heartbeat, blood pressure, fluid balance and body temperature. Functions of the brain are responsible for cognition, emotion, memory, motor learning and other sorts of learning. The brain is primarily made up of two types of cells: glia and neurons.
Skeletal muscle	Skeletal muscle is a type of striated muscle, attached to the skeleton. They are used to facilitate movement, by applying force to bones and joints; via contraction. They generally contract voluntarily (via nerve stimulation), although they can contract involuntarily.

Hypertension	Hypertension is a medical condition where the blood pressure in the arteries is chronically elevated. Persistent hypertension is one of the risk factors for strokes, heart attacks, heart failure and arterial aneurysm, and is a leading cause of chronic renal failure.
Obesity	The state of being more than 20 percent above the average weight for a person of one's height is called obesity.
Statistics	Statistics is a type of data analysis which practice includes the planning, summarizing, and interpreting of observations of a system possibly followed by predicting or forecasting of future events based on a mathematical model of the system being observed.
Statistic	A statistic is an observable random variable of a sample.
Variable	A variable refers to a measurable factor, characteristic, or attribute of an individual or a system.
Coronary heart disease	Coronary heart disease is the end result of the accumulation of atheromatous plaques within the walls of the arteries that supply the myocardium (the muscle of the heart).
Structured interview	Structured interview refers to an interview in which the questions are set out in a prescribed fashion for the interviewer. It assists professionals in making diagnostic decisions based upon standardized criteria.
Plaques	Plaques refer to small, round areas composed of remnants of lost neurons and beta-amyloid, a waxy protein deposit; present in the brains of patients with Alzheimer's disease.
Chronic	Chronic refers to a relatively long duration, usually more than a few months.
Arthritis	Arthritis is a group of conditions that affect the health of the bone joints in the body. Arthritis can be caused from strains and injuries caused by repetitive motion, sports, overexertion, and falls. Unlike the autoimmune diseases, it largely affects older people and results from the degeneration of joint cartilage.
Lymphocyte	A lymphocyte is a type of white blood cell involved in the human body's immune system. There are two broad categories, namely T cells and B cells. The lymphocyte play an important and integral part of the body's defenses.
Immune response	The body's defensive reaction to invasion by bacteria, viral agents, or other foreign substances is called the immune response.
Alzheimer's disease	Alzheimer's disease is an incurable, degenerative neuropsychiatric disease which results in a pervasive loss of first mental, then physical functioning due to the deterioration of brain tissue.
Control group	A group that does not receive the treatment effect in an experiment is referred to as the control group or sometimes as the comparison group.
Placebo	Placebo refers to a bogus treatment that has the appearance of being genuine.
Baseline	Measure of a particular behavior or process taken before the introduction of the independent variable or treatment is called the baseline.
Self-esteem	Self-esteem refers to a person's subjective appraisal of himself or herself as intrinsically positive or negative to some degree.
Punishment	Punishment is the addtion of a stimulus that reduces the frequency of a response, or the removal of a stimulus that results in a reduction of the response.
Mood disorder	A mood disorder is a condition where the prevailing emotional mood is distorted or inappropriate to the circumstances.
Major depression	Major depression is characterized by a severely depressed mood that persists for at least two

Chapter 14. Health

133

Go to **Cram101.com** for the Practice Tests for this Chapter.
And, **NEVER** highlight a book again!

weeks. Episodes of depression may start suddenly or slowly and can occur several times through a person's life. The disorder may be categorized as "single episode" or "recurrent" depending on whether previous episodes have been experienced before.

Psychological disorder	Mental processes and/or behavior patterns that cause emotional distress and/or substantial impairment in functioning is a psychological disorder.
Adolescence	The period of life bounded by puberty and the assumption of adult responsibilities is adolescence.
Learned helplessness	Learned helplessness is a description of the effect of inescapable positive punishment (such as electrical shock) on animal (and by extension, human) behavior.
Attitude	An enduring mental representation of a person, place, or thing that evokes an emotional response and related behavior is called attitude.
Personality	Personality refers to the pattern of enduring characteristics that differentiates a person, the patterns of behaviors that make each individual unique.
Hardiness	A personality characteristic associated with a lower rate of stress-related illness, consisting of three components: commitment, challenge, and control is hardiness.
Perception	Perception is the process of acquiring, interpreting, selecting, and organizing sensory information.
Self-efficacy	Self-efficacy is the belief that one has the capabilities to execute the courses of actions required to manage prospective situations.
Migraine	Migraine is a form of headache, usually very intense and disabling. It is a neurologic disease.
Placebo effect	The placebo effect is the phenomenon that a patient's symptoms can be alleviated by an otherwise ineffective treatment, apparently because the individual expects or believes that it will work.
Sensation	Sensation is the first stage in the chain of biochemical and neurologic events that begins with the impinging of a stimulus upon the receptor cells of a sensory organ, which then leads to perception, the mental state that is reflected in statements like "I see a uniformly blue wall."
Cardiovascular disease	Cardiovascular disease refers to afflictions in the mechanisms, including the heart, blood vessels, and their controllers, that are responsible for transporting blood to the body's tissues and organs. Psychological factors may play important roles in such diseases and their treatments.
Questionnaire	A self-report method of data collection or clinical assessment method in which the individual being studied checks off items on a printed list, answers multiple-choice questions, or writes out answers to essay questions aimed at producing a selfdescription is called questionnaire.
Counselor	A counselor is a mental health professional who specializes in helping people with problems not involving serious mental disorders.
Emotion-focused coping	Lazarus' emotion-focused coping describes individuals' response to stress demonstrated in an emotional manner, especially using defensive methods.
Longitudinal study	Longitudinal study is a type of developmental study in which the same group of participants is followed and measured for an extended period of time, often years.
Health psychology	The field of psychology that studies the relationships between psychological factors and the prevention and treatment of physical illness is called health psychology.

Compensation	In personaility, compensation, according to Adler, is an effort to overcome imagined or real inferiorities by developing one's abilities.
Rape	Rape is a crime where the victim is forced into sexual activity, in particular sexual penetration, against his or her will.
Trauma	Trauma refers to a severe physical injury or wound to the body caused by an external force, or a psychological shock having a lasting effect on mental life.
Denial	Denial is a psychological defense mechanism in which a person faced with a fact that is uncomfortable or painful to accept rejects it instead, insisting that it is not true despite what may be overwhelming evidence.
Problem-focused coping	Lazarus' problem-focused coping is a strategy used by individuals who face their troubles and try to solve them.
Suppression	Suppression is the defense mechanism where a memory is deliberately forgotten.
Consciousness	The awareness of the sensations, thoughts, and feelings being experienced at a given moment is called consciousness.
Psychological test	Psychological test refers to a standardized measure of a sample of a person's behavior.
Correlation	A statistical technique for determining the degree of association between two or more variables is referred to as correlation.
Psychotherapy	Psychotherapy is a set of techniques based on psychological principles intended to improve mental health, emotional or behavioral issues.
Sexual abuse	Sexual abuse is a term used to describe non- consentual sexual relations between two or more parties which are considered criminally and/or morally offensive.
Catharsis	Catharsis has been adopted by modern psychotherapy as the act of giving expression to deep emotions often associated with events in the individuals past which have never before been adequately expressed.
Insight	Insight refers to a sudden awareness of the relationships among various elements that had previously appeared to be independent of one another.
Confederate	Someone who is posing as a participant in an experiment but is actually assisting the experimenter is a confederate.
Alcoholism	A disorder that involves long-term, repeated, uncontrolled, compulsive, and excessive use of alcoholic beverages and that impairs the drinker's health and work and social relationships is called alcoholism.
Self-awareness	Realization that one's existence and functioning are separate from those of other people and things is called self-awareness.
Script	A schema, or behavioral sequence, for an event is called a script. It is a form of schematic organization, with real-world events organized in terms of temporal and causal relations between component acts.
Self-concept	Self-concept refers to domain-specific evaluations of the self where a domain may be academics, athletics, etc.
Feedback loop	A system in which the hypothalamus, pituitary gland, and gonads regulate each other's functioning through a series of hormonal messages is a feedback loop.
Feedback	Feedback refers to information returned to a person about the effects a response has had.
Aerobic exercise	Aerobic exercise is a type of exercise in which muscles draw on oxygen in the blood as well

Go to **Cram101.com** for the Practice Tests for this Chapter.

as fats and glucose, that increase cardiovascular endurance.

Meditation	Meditation usually refers to a state in which the body is consciously relaxed and the mind is allowed to become calm and focused.
Physiological changes	Alterations in heart rate, blood pressure, perspiration, and other involuntary responses are physiological changes.
Proactive coping	Proactive coping are efforts or actions taken in advance of a potentially stressful situation to prevent its occurrence or to minimize its consequences.
Social support	Social Support is the physical and emotional comfort given by family, friends, co-workers and others. Research has identified three main types of social support: emotional, practical, sharing points of view.
Social isolation	Social isolation refers to a type of loneliness that occurs when a person lacks a sense of integrated involvement. Being deprived of participation in a group or community involving companionship, shared interests, organized activities, and meaningful roles causes a person to feel alone.
Simulation	A simulation is an imitation of some real device or state of affairs. Simulation attempts to represent certain features of the behavior of a physical or abstract system by the behavior of another system.
Cortisol	Cortisol is a corticosteroid hormone that is involved in the response to stress; it increases blood pressure and blood sugar levels and suppresses the immune system. Synthetic cortisol, also known as hydrocortisone, is used as a drug mainly to fight allergies and inflammation.
Social role	Social role refers to expected behavior patterns associated with particular social positions.
Social skills	Social skills are skills used to interact and communicate with others to assist status in the social structure and other motivations.
Cognitive dissonance	Cognitive dissonance is a state of opposition between cognitions. Contradicting cognitions serve as a driving force that compel the mind to acquire or invent new thoughts or beliefs, or to modify existing beliefs, so as to minimize the amount of dissonance between cognitions.
Habit	A habit is a response that has become completely separated from its eliciting stimulus. Early learning theorists used the term to describe S-R associations, however not all S-R associations become a habit, rather many are extinguished after reinforcement is withdrawn.
Homosexual	Homosexual refers to a sexual orientation characterized by aesthetic attraction, romantic love, and sexual desire exclusively for members of the same sex or gender identity.
Semen	Semen is a fluid that contains spermatozoa. It is secreted by the gonads of males for the fertilization of female ova.
Social psychology	Social psychology is the study of the nature and causes of human social behavior, with an emphasis on how people think towards each other and how they relate to each other.
Incentive	An incentive is what is expected once a behavior is performed. An incentive acts as a reinforcer.
Norms	In testing, standards of test performance that permit the comparison of one person's score on the test to the scores of others who have taken the same test are referred to as norms.
Modeling	A type of behavior learned through observation of others demonstrating the same behavior is modeling.
Parkinson's disease	Parkinson's disease is a neurodegenerative disease of the substantia nigra (an area in the basal ganglia of the brain). The disease involves a progressive movement disorder of the extrapyramidal system, which controls and adjusts communication between neurons in the brain

and muscles in the human body. It commonly involves depression and disturbances of sensory systems.

Theories	Theories are logically self-consistent models or frameworks describing the behavior of a certain natural or social phenomenon. They are broad explanations and predictions concerning phenomena of interest.
False-consensus effect	The tendency for people to overestimate the extent to which others share their opinions, attributes, and behaviors is called the false-consensus effect.
Physical attractiveness	Physical attractiveness is the perception of an individual as physically beautiful by other people.
Social comparison theory	Social comparison theory is the idea that individuals learn about and assess themselves by comparison with other people. Social psychological research shows that individuals tend to lean more toward social comparisons in situations that are ambiguous.
Social comparison	Social comparison theory is the idea that individuals learn about and assess themselves by comparison with other people. Research shows that individuals tend to lean more toward social comparisons in situations that are ambiguous.
Identical twins	Identical twins occur when a single egg is fertilized to form one zygote (monozygotic) but the zygote then divides into two separate embryos. The two embryos develop into foetuses sharing the same womb. Monozygotic twins are genetically identical unless there has been a mutation in development, and they are almost always the same gender.

CPSIA information can be obtained at www.ICGtesting.com
Printed in the USA
BVOW10s2359010614

355053BV00001B/11/A